# Academic Careers for Experimental Computer Scientists and Engineers

• • • • • • • • • • • • • • • • • • • • • • •

Committee on Academic Careers for
Experimental Computer Scientists

Computer Science and Telecommunications Board

Commission on Physical Sciences, Mathematics,
and Applications

National Research Co

National Academy Press
Washington, D.C.   1994

NOTICE: The project that is the subject of this report was approved by the Governing Board of the National Research Council, whose members are drawn from the councils of the National Academy of Sciences, the National Academy of Engineering, and the Institute of Medicine. The members of the committee responsible for the report were chosen for their special competences and with regard for appropriate balance.

This report has been reviewed by a group other than the authors according to procedures approved by a Report Review Committee consisting of members of the National Academy of Sciences, the National Academy of Engineering, and the Institute of Medicine.

The National Academy of Sciences is a private, nonprofit, self-perpetuating society of distinguished scholars engaged in scientific and engineering research, dedicated to the furtherance of science and technology and to their use for the general welfare. Upon the authority of the charter granted to it by the Congress in 1863, the Academy has a mandate that requires it to advise the federal government on scientific and technical matters. Dr. Bruce Alberts is president of the National Academy of Sciences.

The National Academy of Engineering was established in 1964, under the charter of the National Academy of Sciences, as a parallel organization of outstanding engineers. It is autonomous in its administration and in the selection of its members, sharing with the National Academy of Sciences the responsibility for advising the federal government. The National Academy of Engineering also sponsors engineering programs aimed at meeting national needs, encourages education and research, and recognizes the superior achievements of engineers. Dr. Robert M. White is president of the National Academy of Engineering.

The Institute of Medicine was established in 1970 by the National Academy of Sciences to secure the services of eminent members of appropriate professions in the examination of policy matters pertaining to the health of the public. The Institute acts under the responsibility given to the National Academy of Sciences by its congressional charter to be an adviser to the federal government and, upon its own initiative, to identify issues of medical care, research, and education. Dr. Kenneth I. Shine is president of the Institute of Medicine.

The National Research Council was organized by the National Academy of Sciences in 1916 to associate the broad community of science and technology with the Academy's purposes of furthering knowledge and advising the federal government. Functioning in accordance with general policies determined by the Academy, the Council has become the principal operating agency of both the National Academy of Sciences and the National Academy of Engineering in providing services to the government, the public, and the scientific and engineering communities. The Council is administered jointly by both Academies and the Institute of Medicine. Dr. Bruce Alberts and Dr. Robert M. White are chairman and vice chairman, respectively, of the National Research Council.

Support for this project was provided by the National Science Foundation (under Grant No. CDA-9024633) and core funds of the Computer Science and Telecommunications Board.

Any opinions, findings, conclusions, or recommendations expressed in this material are those of the authoring committee and do not necessarily reflect the views of the National Science Foundation.

Library of Congress Catalog Card Number 93-84437
International Standard Book Number 0-309-04931-8

Additional copies of this report are available from:

National Academy Press
2101 Constitution Avenue, NW
Box 285
Washington, DC  20055
800-624-6242
202-334-3313 (in the Washington Metropolitan Area)

B-158

# Preface

Experimental computer science and engineering (ECSE) is the fundamental underpinning of the computer hardware and software that drive the information age. The national importance of research in this field led the National Science Foundation (NSF) to ask the Computer Science and Telecommunications Board (CSTB) of the National Research Council to conduct a study of career tracks for experimental computer scientists and engineers in academia. NSF's concern was motivated by the observation that the challenges faced by experimental computer scientists and engineers in academia, especially those of being evaluated and of creating appropriate research environments, may be different from those encountered by their more theoretically oriented counterparts.

The CSTB Committee on Academic Careers for Experimental Computer Scientists deliberated on this subject for a year. While it drew on its own experience and contacts within the field, it also made considerable use of several informal surveys of the ECSE community, sent out with the cooperation of the Computing Research Association. Appendix A contains a description of the survey methodology. In addition, the committee solicited input at an open workshop held at the biennial Snowbird meeting of Ph.D.-granting computer science and engineering department chairs in July 1992.

Beyond explaining the need for conducting ECSE research at universities, characterizing the unique nature of the field, and describing successful experimental research, this report focuses on the challenges faced by faculty who wish to be successful experimentalists. Accordingly, the report is directed to university faculty and administrators, as well as government policymakers and industry leaders (who employ experimental computer scientists and engineers and depend on their intellectual output).

Made available recently, two other reports that address some of the issues discussed in this report are the Liskov report[1] and the record of the Computing Research Association Workshop on Academic Careers for Women (in computer science and engineering).[2] The Liskov report was concerned with how to improve research in experimental computer science by identifying problems in the field and proposing solutions. The second report unfortunately came to the attention of the committee too late for it to be referenced in the main body of this report. Although it was aimed at women with careers in the field, much of the advice and commentary applies to men in the field as well.

This report deals primarily with the career tracks of regular faculty members in experimental computer science and engineering, i.e., faculty who are eligible for tenure and have a mix of regular research and teaching responsibilities. This group constitutes the largest number of experimental computer scientists and engineers in academia. Regular faculty positions are not the only possible academic careers, but all other paths share one primary characteristic: positions other than those of regular faculty members are generally contingent on the availability of outside funding (so-called soft money). This dependence on outside funding implies that a research grant or contract provides the primary support for such a person; accordingly, his or her responsibilities are, in contrast to those of regular faculty members, avowedly in the research domain, although he or she may have a teaching opportunity from time to time. Academic positions funded by soft money are by definition somewhat tenuous; at institutions with large ECSE research programs, holders of such positions have greater flexibility to switch among ongoing projects. Because most universities are generally willing to hire individuals for nonprofessorial

---

[1] Liskov, Barbara. 1992. *Report on Workshop on Research in Experimental Computer Science.* MIT/LCS/TR-540. Laboratory for Computer Science, Massachusetts Institute of Technology, Cambridge.

[2] Edited transcripts of this workshop are available by anonymous FTP from the site "ics.uci.edu" and are contained in the directory "pub/mentoring-workshop." This workshop was held at the Federated Computing Research Conference at San Diego, California, on May 15, 1993.

positions when outside funding is available, the committee concluded that the truly knotty issues are those faced by the regular faculty member in ECSE.

The comments and criticisms of reviewers of early drafts of this report are gratefully acknowledged. Of course, the findings, conclusions, and judgments of this report are solely the responsibility of the committee.

CSTB will be glad to receive comments on this report. Please send them via e-mail to CSTB@NAS.EDU, or via regular mail to CSTB, National Academy of Sciences, 2101 Constitution Avenue, Washington, DC 20418.

# Contents

# Executive Summary

Experimental computer science and engineering (ECSE) is the fundamental underpinning of the computer hardware and software that drive the information age. Many widely known computer advancements of the 1980s trace their origins to ECSE research. Examples are known to the average user—reduced instruction set computers, window systems, relational databases—but many more are hidden inside systems, making them faster, more efficient, or more functional, or they are part of the technological infrastructure that supports the rapid innovation so characteristic of the computer field. Experimental work is also an essential intellectual element of the computer science and engineering (CS&E) discipline that enriches research and teaching in the field.

Industry and universities both play major roles in supporting ECSE. ECSE research in academia in particular plays an important role in ensuring an adequate diversity of technical ideas out of which marketable products can emerge. Moreover, performing ECSE research in the university environment enriches the educational mission of universities and keeps faculty members current in the discipline. The importance of academic ECSE led the National Science Foundation (NSF) to request a study by the Computer Science and Telecommunications Board of academic career tracks for practitioners in the field. The NSF request was motivated by the concern that experimental computer scientists and engineers may face special chal-

*1*

lenges in being evaluated and in creating appropriate research environments, although some top-ranked universities have met these challenges quite well.

## THE NATURE OF EXPERIMENTAL COMPUTER SCIENCE AND ENGINEERING

Experimental computer science and engineering (ECSE) is a synthetic discipline in the sense that it studies phenomena that are entirely the product of human creation. Many interesting computational phenomena—processes, algorithms, or mechanisms that manipulate or transform information—are too complex to understand on the basis of direct analysis from first principles. For example, an algorithm may have many complicated states, or a process may involve time-dependent interactions of many subprocesses. For all practical purposes, such complex phenomena can be understood only on the basis of empirical observation.

Thus, ECSE refers to the creation of, or the experimentation with or on, computational *artifacts*. Often artifacts are hardware systems (such as computers) or software systems (such as text editors), but the term includes graphic images or animations, robots, or test and benchmark suites. When computational processes, algorithms, or mechanisms are implemented in an artifact, the behavior of the system and the interaction of its components can be observed in action. In general, when the computational phenomenon is complex, an artifact that embodies the idea will also be complex and will have many component parts.

In ECSE, artifacts may be the subject of a study, the apparatus for a study, or both. Artifacts often embody a substantial portion of the intellectual contribution of ECSE research, and their creation represents a significant intellectual effort.

Artifacts serve at least three primary purposes in ECSE. A given implementation can seek performance or seek improvement and enhancement of prior implementations (proof of performance), demonstrate that a particular configuration of ideas or an approach achieves its objectives (proof of concept), or demonstrate a fundamentally new computing phenomenon (proof of existence).

Computing artifacts are malleable and versatile. Unlike other machines, computers are "universal," meaning that within broad limits, whatever one machine can do, all machines can do. Although this property is extremely convenient in many respects, it implies the lack of an a priori limit on the functionality of computers, which feeds ever-expanding expectations for their capabilities.

The construction of computing artifacts is not strongly coupled to theoretical computer science. Unlike the more traditional sciences (e.g., physics) in which the interplay and coupling between experiment and theory are rather tight, an "experiment" in ECSE generally does not verify a prediction from theoretical computer science or rely heavily on a model developed theoretically. The reason is that the complexity of most real computing problems precludes the direct application of analysis: a problem can be made theoretically tractable only by abstracting so extensively that the problem that emerges may not capture the essence of the original problem.

Because ECSE is strongly coupled to technology, the availability of a given technology may well determine the feasibility of a good and innovative idea. The use of cutting-edge technology for a project subjects it to hazards such as instability, errors, and delays, whereas the use of a stable, mature technology carries the risk of obsolescence before the project is finished.

## ECSE AND THE ACADEMIC ENVIRONMENT

The characteristics of ECSE have a major impact on how ECSE faculty must go about their work. An academic career in ECSE resembles one in other science or engineering disciplines only in outline (including teaching, advising students, writing papers and proposals, conducting research, serving on committees, and so on). The most substantive difference, perhaps, concerns how research is evaluated. Because ECSE is fundamentally a synthetic discipline, it is straightforward to create a new computational phenomenon or an alternate implementation of a concept. Yet doing so does not automatically constitute an intellectual contribution. Rather, whatever has been created must be shown to be better than some alternative. In research in theoretical computer science, the key question is, Has the proposition been proved? In contrast, the key questions in evaluating ECSE research include, Does the idea provide a new and more useful capability or greater functionality? and, Is it faster or more efficient?

Box ES.1 describes how the mouse—a device for human-computer interaction—can be evaluated in these terms and thus found to be a success story in ECSE research. Other artifacts that emerge from ECSE research may not have had as illustrious a history, but they can also be significant.

Artifacts in a proof-of-performance role demonstrate that they are better because they are objectively faster or consume fewer resources. But it may be harder to prove the greater worth of artifacts

---

### BOX ES.1 The Mouse as ECSE Research

The computer mouse is used as a pointing device in human-computer interaction. The mouse was created by Douglas Engelbart at SRI as one of several human-computer communication devices. Although it was described in full technical detail and careful studies were made of its utility, many computer scientists recall first appreciating the power and significance of the invention, not from the published record, but from a film that Engelbart produced, showing the mouse in action. The demonstration of the device conveyed the essence of the new phenomenon beyond any amount of description of how, or how well, it worked.

In the ECSE research context, the concepts embodied in the mouse can be evaluated as follows:

- The mouse falls within the scope of ECSE, having mechanical, electronic, and software components concerned with human-computer interfaces.
- The mouse concepts fundamentally improve the functionality of the human-computer interface.
- The concepts were shown to be better quantitatively.
- The mouse has had significant impact, as witnessed by a variety of subsequent implementations, improvements, and applications, as well as its widespread use.

This lineage and history associate the mouse with a proof-of-existence role and place it squarely in the ranks of successful ECSE research.

---

serving a proof-of-concept or a proof-of-existence role, because the advancement may be qualitative, as in increased functionality. In this context, what is considered better may depend on subjective human judgments.

The production of computing artifacts depends on a substantial infrastructure. Equipment needs are generally well understood, although few outside the computer fields realize just how quickly "state-of-the-art" equipment loses its cutting edge and utility for research. Equipment also requires space that must generally be specially equipped with power and air-conditioning capacity not found in standard office or teaching space. Experimental software systems often require dedicated or special-purpose hardware and cannot make use of the general-purpose computing environment that already exists in the department, school, or university.

Advanced graduate students are critical to ECSE research. Systems projects involve a great deal of detailed design and implementation, and because the artifacts involved in ECSE research must by definition be created from concepts (rather than blueprints), the students constructing them must have appropriate background, skills, and knowledge.

Larger ECSE projects require support from technicians and other staff who maintain the research environment and provide implementation assistance. Such staff free graduate students to focus more of their time on the intellectually significant parts of the implementation project and less on the more routine or lower-level (although necessary) components of system building.

Large- or even medium-scale ECSE research also requires collaborative or team effort, and all scales of research are likely to incorporate the previous efforts of others. Researchers can save valuable time and resources by using public domain and even commercial system components. More importantly, an individual researcher can have more impact by working with a team than would be possible by working alone and from scratch. Especially for large efforts, collaboration is essential because the subsystems of an artifact are often so specialized that other expertise is needed.

Funding, which is important to researchers in any field, must be sufficient to cover the long time horizons and large demands on resources that characterize ECSE research. However, programs intended to support junior faculty who have not yet established their professional reputations (e.g., the NSF Young Investigator program and the Research Initiation Awards program of the Computer and Information Science and Engineering Directorate of NSF) are highly competitive, and so only a few faculty members receive such support in their first year after graduation. Thus, new ECSE faculty are not likely to have research support based on their own research ideas during the early years of their careers and may well have to rely during this time on "start-up" funding provided by the hiring school.

Finally, the time demands on ECSE faculty are inflated by the nature of the field. For example, given the time needed to build a research team and a laboratory, even a very good assistant professor in ECSE may have only one completed Ph.D. student and/or one major completed project before a tenure decision is made. Because the dissemination of artifacts is an essential medium through which research knowledge in ECSE diffuses into the community, the six-year probationary period for an assistant professor may be too short to establish a reputation in the field.

ECSE researchers share their software, provide access (via Internet) to their experimental computers, and distribute their data files. Disseminating by means of artifacts allows research colleagues to acquire a working knowledge of an experimentalist's accomplishments that is deeper and more extensive than would be possible simply by reading journal papers. In some cases (e.g., in the display of a graphic animation that one must see develop in time), there is no adequate written alternative to observing the animation in action.

The ECSE research community depends heavily on conferences to communicate new knowledge, and conferences are widely regarded as the preferred medium for maximizing the intellectual impact of ECSE research. However, the tenure and promotion process at many universities does not give conference presentations and publications a weight appropriate to their significance in the field, preferring instead publications in archival journals.

The focus of ECSE on artifacts has often led to a tension between theoretical and experimental computer scientists. Although the tension seems not to manifest itself in some departments, in others it appears to have caused experimental or theoretical work to be misunderstood and underappreciated by researchers in the opposite camp. This has obvious implications for junior faculty members in departments in which the senior faculty are primarily of a "different stripe"; their readiness for promotion and tenure may not be evaluated according to the standards for quality and the criteria for success that apply to their research specialty.

## PROVIDING A NURTURING ENVIRONMENT FOR ECSE FACULTY

Some schools, typically those with large groups of experimentalists, have fostered highly supportive environments for ECSE faculty. However, many more schools—perhaps because of their smaller size or particular history—have few experimentalists and little experimental activity under way. In such schools, many ECSE faculty perceive the career environment to be difficult or hostile.

One key element of a positive environment for ECSE is the availability of a mentor for junior faculty. Mentors should provide advice on issues such as publication, funding sources, collaboration, choice of problems, and logistics. For example, a mentor might suggest conferences or journals in which publication would bring maximum exposure or prestige, funding agencies most likely to support a junior faculty member's work, senior professors at other institutions with whom to collaborate, and ways to structure projects so that intermediate results could be made available.

Advocacy of a faculty member's interest to higher authorities (e.g., university administrations) is also essential. Advocates would, for example, argue the case for obtaining review letters from appropriate parties, explain key characteristics of ECSE to those outside the field, accumulate evidence of the impact of the junior faculty member's work, and document the structure and stature of the literature (e.g., which conferences and journals are respected, prestigious, and well refereed).

In addition, department and university evaluators must strive to use standards and criteria for tenure and promotion decisions that normally characterize productive work in the ECSE discipline, rather than standards that may be applicable to more traditional academic disciplines, taking care not to exclude meaningful evidence of achievement (e.g., artifacts with substantial impact on the ECSE community) simply because it is nonstandard.

With respect to the important letter-writing process in tenure and promotion, the primary criteria in selecting potential letter writers should be their stature in the field and their familiarity with the candidate's work. Factors such as the letter writer's institutional location or status as a collaborator should not be reasons for excluding letters. In particular, because views from industry may be important for judging the impact of ECSE work, letters from individuals in industry or government laboratories should not be arbitrarily limited, and they should carry equal weight to those of similarly qualified and reputable individuals in academia. Similarly, eschewing letters from collaborators in a field as intrinsically collaborative as ECSE is to eliminate some of the best possible input regarding a candidate's intellectual capability, creativity, and originality.

More generally, universities should recognize that an experimentalist being considered for tenure or promotion may have fewer publications (and predominantly conference publications), nonstandard forms of dissemination (e.g., distribution of software artifacts), substantial amounts of collaborative research, and few graduate students completed, and yet still be a spectacular researcher. A judgment should be based on the presence or absence of the following:

- One or more computational impact-producing artifacts completed;
- Research results disseminated to and used by the community;
- A reputation for novel systems solutions or ingenious experiments; and
- A filled or filling pipeline of well-trained graduate students.

It is the responsibility of the candidate to achieve distinction. It is the responsibility of the department and institution to recognize and reward it.

Departments can improve the environment for ECSE faculty by providing technical staff support and laboratory space. Start-up packages for new assistant professors in ECSE comparable to those received by new experimentalists in other departments would enable them to begin research more quickly. Providing opportunities for junior faculty members to teach advanced seminars in which graduate students can receive needed training in preparation for joining a research project would facilitate the building of a research team.

The federal government and industry also have critical roles to play in improving the environment for ECSE in academia. Most importantly, the federal government should realize that a variety of funding structures are needed to support ECSE research, including small, relatively short term grants or contracts that focus primarily on the development of a concept; medium-scale group funding; and large, relatively long term grants or contracts associated with deliverable computing artifacts. Postdoctoral support for new Ph.D.s in ECSE would help to overcome some of the limitations and constraints imposed by the six-year probationary period for assistant professors.

The computer industry can help to enhance the environment for ECSE in academia by establishing collaborative work arrangements with universities, including those that may not be nationally known or recognized. Computer or software companies that interact with such universities and thus expose local CS&E departments to the problems and needs of industry not only foster meaningful collaborative work but also help to produce students who are better informed about these problems. Such students graduating from less well recognized universities may be more likely to work for local computer or software companies. If appropriate nondisclosure agreements can be achieved, industry can also provide access to hardware designs or source codes for various software systems. An academic researcher's access to source code will certainly reduce the time required for him or her to complete an experimental software system and may result in an improved system of direct interest to the owner of the source code.

# 1
# What Is Experimental Computer Science and Engineering?

Computer science is younger than most academic disciplines, and its partitioning into experimental and theoretical components has occurred more recently still. As used in this report, experimental computer science and engineering (ECSE) refers to the building of, or the experimentation with or on, nontrivial hardware or software systems. ECSE as a field is a constituent of the intellectual revolution begun by the invention of the electronic computer in the 1940s and its subsequent commercialization.

Although the building of the first (experimental) computers fits the definition given above, the field did not emerge until perhaps the mid-1960s as an identifiable research discipline distinct from either numerical computation or what has since become known as theoretical computer science. With the need for ECSE faculty greatly exceeding the supply, the Feldman report[1] in 1979 identified the limited availability of computer hardware as the principal constraint on the production of Ph.D.s in the field. The National Science Foundation (NSF) initiated the highly successful Coordinated Experimental Research (CER) program as a remedy. Today, many schools on the

---

[1] Feldman, Jerome A., and William R. Sutherland. 1979. "Rejuvenating Experimental Computer Science," *Communications of the ACM* (September):497-502.

Forsythe list[2] have one or more experimentalists, and more than half of the members of some departments are ECSE faculty.

Experimental computer science and engineering programs at U.S. universities differ significantly. Some schools, typically those with large groups of experimentalists, are quite able to build and maintain the faculty and infrastructure necessary to conduct significant experimental research. Highly trained graduates are produced, and technology is created that is valuable to national competitiveness as well as important for its scholarly content. Junior faculty are mentored to be successful at promotion time. At these schools, the tenure and promotion process seems to accommodate the particular characteristics (enumerated below) of experimental research that complicate an academic ECSE career.

However, a much larger number of schools—perhaps characterized by their smaller size or accidents of their development—have few experimentalists and little experimental activity under way. These schools include some that otherwise have strong reputations. Many such schools present a career environment that new assistant professors in ECSE often perceive as difficult or hostile. Many ECSE faculty at these "nonexperimental" schools—untenured and tenured alike—described for the committee the difficulties of creating and maintaining research environments appropriate for their needs; further, they reported a strong belief that promotion required them to do theoretical research as assistant professors in order to gain the respect of senior faculty and produce enough publications to meet the tests of the "paper counters" within the department, college, and university.

To the extent that these latter views are valid, there are several major implications. In the absence of a fair and balanced academic reward system for ECSE faculty, promising and talented experimental computer scientists and engineers may well forsake academic life in disproportionate numbers, leaving an academic community unduly weighted toward theoretical work and increasingly irrelevant to computing practice. Such a shift would serve students poorly, since a balanced education includes instruction in the state-of-the-art technologies that are essential for productive careers. Such instruction is most effectively provided by faculty engaged in cutting-edge experimental research. Moreover, because academic research in ECSE is critical to the continued technological preeminence of the United States

---

[2] The set of academic departments offering a doctorate in computer science or computer engineering is known in the field as the "Forsythe list" after the late George Forsythe, a professor of Computer Science at Stanford University, who originally compiled it.

in computer hardware and software, the competitive advantages that derive from such research may be dulled if that research infrastructure is weakened.

## ORGANIZATION AND SCOPE OF THIS REPORT

The remainder of this chapter sets experimental computer science and engineering in context, defines it, describes defining characteristics of its research methodologies, and then elaborates on the need to conduct ECSE research at universities. Chapter 2 describes the requirements of academic career development in ECSE, along with the infrastructure and support needs of experimental computer scientists and engineers. Chapter 3 deals with the educational dimensions of academic ECSE. Chapter 4 addresses both the philosophy of evaluating ECSE research and some of the practicalities related to such evaluation. Chapter 5 describes the committee's judgment about the characteristics of a positive environment for academic ECSE. Chapter 6 describes the special needs and concerns of non-doctorate-granting and less recognized institutions. Chapter 7 provides the key findings and recommendations of this report.

The scope of this report was limited by the committee's charge and the resources available to the committee. In particular, no systematic attempt was made to survey the entire computer science and engineering community or to characterize all institutions in which ECSE research is undertaken. Rather, the committee developed its insights through its own deliberations and its informal, although extensive, contacts with other experimental computer scientists and engineers. As a check on its insights and conclusions, the committee made substantial use of several informal surveys sent to the ECSE community with the cooperation of the Computing Research Association (CRA);[3] these surveys are referred to collectively throughout this report as "the CRA-CSTB survey." Appendix A describes the survey instruments in more detail. Appendix B provides a quantitative comparison between two modes of publication: journals and conferences.

The committee did not examine in detail analogous problems in other disciplines. It may be that many of the problems, real or perceived, discussed in this report are also encountered by biotechnologists,

---

[3] The Computing Research Association is a service organization for the computer science and engineering (CS&E) research community. It is supported primarily by academic CS&E departments, whether doctorate granting or not.

materials scientists, and other academic researchers in scientific or engineering disciplines closely linked to practice. Some comparisons with other fields are given later in this chapter.

## COMPUTER SCIENCE AND ENGINEERING

To set the context for defining *experimental* computer science and engineering in detail (see following section), it is necessary to consider the field of computer science and engineering (CS&E) as a whole. Defining computer science and engineering is not a trivial matter, and multiple definitions exist. Two are considered from the point of view of experimentation.

A recent CSTB report, *Computing the Future*, characterizes CS&E as a field.[4] Although it does not explicitly identify CS&E's experimental components, experimentation is indeed an important aspect of many of the field's subdisciplines.

*Computing the Future* defines the essential intellectual content of the field in the following terms:

> [C]omputer scientists and engineers focus on information, on the ways of representing and processing information, and on the machines and systems that perform these tasks. (p. 19)

It then identifies the key intellectual themes of the field as algorithmic thinking, information representation, and computer programs. Furthermore, the report cites accomplishments in five subdisciplines: (1) systems and architectures; (2) programming languages, compilers, and software engineering; (3) artificial intelligence; (4) computer graphics and user interfaces; and (5) algorithms and computational complexity. Although each of these subdisciplines has an experimental and a theoretical component, all but the last have been domains of intensive experimental research.

Another description of the field, "Computing as a Discipline" (also known as the Denning report), takes a different approach to defining the field, which has both strengths and flaws with respect to experimental research.[5] The report enumerates subareas of the field, which is both inclusive and respectful of natural partitionings of the discipline (Box 1.1). The report then classifies the content of each of

---

[4] Computer Science and Telecommunications Board. 1992. *Computing the Future.* National Academy Press, Washington, D.C.

[5] Denning, Peter, Douglas E. Comer, David Gries, Michael C. Mulder, Allen Tucker, Joe Turner, and Paul R. Young. 1989. "Computing as a Discipline," *Communications of the ACM* 32(1):9-23.

---

**BOX 1.1  A Taxonomy of Computer Science**

Algorithms and data structures
Programming languages
Computer architecture
Numeric and symbolic computation
Operating systems
Software engineering
Databases and information retrieval
Artificial intelligence and robotics
Human-computer interaction

SOURCE: Denning, Peter, Douglas E. Comer, David Gries, Michael C. Mulder, Allen Tucker, Joe Turner, and Paul R. Young. 1989. "Computing as a Discipline," *Communications of the ACM* 32(1):9-23.

---

the subareas via "three basic processes—theory, abstraction, and design—that are used by the disciplinary subareas to accomplish their goals." However, this tripartite classification ignores the role of experimentation.

For example, either by dictionary definition or common usage in the field, performance evaluation—the activity of understanding how well hardware or software systems perform—would not be described as theory, abstraction, or design. It is experimentation, and it is an important subdiscipline of ECSE. This and other experimental topics cannot be found in the taxonomy. Indeed, constructing artifacts, a defining property of ECSE as explained below, is not included in the trinity. The Denning report must continually append to the design component the phrase "and implementational issues" to make the connection to constructing artifacts. A formulation recognizing an experimental and a theoretical component in each topic area might have been more descriptive of the field.

For the purposes of this report, CS&E is defined by the above-quoted "representing and processing information" definition from *Computing the Future*. The topic areas of *Computing the Future* or the Denning report, broadly construed, can serve as a high-level decomposition of the field. Further, most phenomena in CS&E are being studied by using both theoretical and experimental methodologies.

Partitioning the field into experimental and theoretical topics is therefore difficult.[6] To the extent that any research meets the definition of ECSE in the next section, the findings of this report apply.

## DEFINING CHARACTERISTICS OF ECSE

Experimental computer science and engineering was defined in the opening paragraph of this chapter as "the building of, or the experimentation with or on, nontrivial hardware or software systems." Although sufficient for an introduction, this one-sentence definition is not precise enough to describe the field exactly. Better definitions would use terms such as *computational artifact* that presuppose an understanding of the field that would obviate the need for a definition. Moreover, they would assume an appreciation of subtle distinctions such as the differences between the nature of experimentation in ECSE and experimentation in physics or biology. Thus, a detailed description of ECSE's characterizing features is presented before returning to the matter of a succinct definition at the end of this section. In addition, because subtle distinctions can be appreciated only after the overall context is understood, the discussion of artifacts is presented in a general fashion, with additional fine (but still important) points raised in the section immediately following this.

Experimental computer science and engineering is defined here in terms of six essential characteristics that, if not unique individually, collectively define a unique field of intellectual depth directed toward understanding diverse phenomena. Perhaps the most critical property is that ECSE focuses on computational artifacts such as hardware or software systems. However, to introduce artifacts properly requires that the synthetic nature of the discipline be treated first. After its synthetic nature is discussed and artifacts are introduced, four properties of experimental research are covered—the complexity of artifacts, their dependence on technology, the universality of the phenomena, and the nonreliance on theory.

---

[6] In *Computing the Future* (1992, p. 194), the definition of theoretical computer science is discussed in "A Note on Terminology." Although the assertion that theory is usually construed too narrowly is certainly true, the revised definition, "all nonexperimental work in CS&E intended to build mathematical foundations and models for describing, explaining, and understanding various aspects of computing," is somewhat vague because experimentation could equally be defined as "all nontheoretical work . . . ." In fact, formulating models for describing, explaining, and understanding various aspects of computing in whatever form is fundamental to the field as a whole, whether the research is experimental or theoretical in nature.

## ECSE Is a Synthetic Discipline

Experimental computer science and engineering shares with other branches of CS&E the fact that it is largely a synthetic discipline. That is, the phenomena studied by most practitioners have been created by a person rather than being "given" by nature.[7] There are fundamental truths, just as there are in mathematics, but computers and information processing are entirely the creations of human beings. This synthetic quality comes into contact with physical phenomena at the extremes of the field (e.g., in metal-oxide semiconductor (MOS) technology for chips or in properties of light reflectance in graphics), but generally the subject matter is synthetic.

With few direct physical constraints, the practitioner has wide latitude to be creative. This possibility of being very imaginative and then implementing one's ideas in a working computer system is one of the exciting rewards of ECSE. However, the synthetic property also introduces complications into the field that may not be encountered by researchers in other fields. Examples described below include difficulties in conveying the intangible qualities of very creative research, complications in assessing the contribution embodied in an artifact, and the interrelatedness of experimental systems. The less constrained quality of this synthetic discipline can be at once liberating to the imagination and at odds sometimes with the traditional assumptions of academic career development in the sciences. In later chapters, this point is discussed further.

## ECSE Focuses Primarily on Artifacts

An *artifact* in ECSE is an instance or implementation of one or more computational phenomena. Because the phenomena being studied are processes, algorithms, mechanisms, and the like that manipulate and transform information, the artifact will embody such manipulations and transformations. Examples of artifacts are hardware sys-

---

[7] Computer science and engineering is synthetic in the sense of being man-made. Another sense of "synthetic"—the composition of parts or elements—also applies to the field, as it does to other engineering disciplines, to describe its focus on the organizing principles of systems. The man-made sense is the more significant in terms of characterizing the field. See Simon, Herbert. 1969. *Sciences of the Artificial.* MIT Press, Cambridge, Mass.

Additionally, the committee recognizes the philosophical debate over whether mathematics is invented or discovered. However, a resolution or a detailed discussion of that subject is not appropriate for this report.

tems (such as computers) or software systems (such as text editors). The artifact can be the subject of study, the apparatus with which to conduct the study, or both. It often embodies a substantial portion of the intellectual contribution of experimental research, and its creation represents a significant intellectual effort.

The term *artifact* is often used here and in the field synonymously with electronic hardware or software systems, but it should be construed much more broadly. Thus, in addition to hardware systems such as computers, chips and circuit boards, and software systems, including compilers, editors, expert systems, computer-aided design (CAD) tools, and so on, experimentalists would likely include graphic images and animations, robots, certain hard-to-construct data files including multiprocessor execution traces, test and benchmark suites such as the International Symposium on Circuits and Systems (ISCAS) suite, structural descriptions such as the Utah Tea Pot, and so on.[8] Other things that experimentalists build and study might be classified as artifacts by some, but not all practitioners would agree. Programming languages, architectures, protocols, and methodologies, such as object-oriented programming, the spiral approach to software development, and domino logic, are examples. The definitional issue in some cases derives from the fact that certain artifacts (e.g., an interpreter for Pascal) are implementations of abstractions (e.g., the Pascal programming language), which in turn could be thought of as implementations of some still more abstract concepts (e.g., procedural imperative programming languages). What is the concept and what is the instance? It may depend on how abstractly one thinks; Table 1.1 illustrates one mapping between ideas and artifacts. However, it is unnecessary for the purposes of this report to be perfectly definitive, because the problems outlined below pertaining to the creation and study of artifacts apply to both the narrow and the broad interpretations.

Artifacts are central to ECSE because the phenomena studied— processes, algorithms, mechanisms, and the like—transform information, describe particular behaviors in response to inputs, and generally are very complex in terms of the total number of constituent parts. Such characteristics almost always overwhelm our ability to understand them by direct analysis. They are simply too complex. Moreover, what is often important is the interaction of the parts (i.e.,

---

[8] The ISCAS suite is a set of circuits designed and used to test computer-assisted tools for chip design. The Utah Tea Pot is a geometric description of a china teapot with lid that is used as a standard picture for graphics-rendering algorithms.

TABLE 1.1  Mapping Ideas to Artifacts

| Idea | Artifact |
|------|----------|
| Extra registers to speed context saving on procedure calls | Microprocessor chip with "register window" and a compiler that generates code to use them |
| Avoiding global clock synchronization to speed simulation of parallel machines | A "conservative" simulation that advances individual clocks independently, but only if all earlier events have been completed<br>An "optimistic" simulation that advances individual clocks independently but "rolls back the clock" when it turns out that clock advance was inappropriate |
| Better software engineering methodology | Tools to enforce the methodology<br>Building programs using this methodology |

their dynamic behavior). Both the large number of program or hardware states and the temporal characteristics of the interaction exacerbate the problem of predicting how well a given computational idea will perform on the basis of a purely logical or theoretical analysis. Consequently, the processes, algorithms, and/or mechanisms must be implemented so that the behavior of the system and the interaction of the components can be observed in action.

Artifacts serve three easily identifiable roles in ECSE research, although there are probably others. The somewhat cumbersome but perhaps suggestive names, proof of performance, proof of concept, and proof of existence, will be used for these roles. (Examples are given in Box 1.2, and further discussion of these roles follows.)

### Proof of Performance

An artifact acting in the proof-of-performance role provides an apparatus or testbed for direct measurement and experimentation. The artifact exists or can be constructed, and the results produced are usually quantitative. This is perhaps the most typical artifact of ECSE research.

A good example of an artifact in a proof-of-performance role is the peephole code optimizer.[9] Fraser observed that compilers (i.e.,

---

[9] Fraser, Christopher W. 1979. "A Compact, Machine-Independent Peephole Optimizer," pp. 1-6 in *Proceedings of the Sixth ACM Symposium on the Principles of Programming Languages*, Association of Computing Machinery, New York.

## BOX 1.2   Examples of Artifacts in Different Roles

### Proof of Performance

• The *original RISC prototypes* were built to demonstrate the performance and implementation advantages of what became known as reduced instruction set computers. These implementations were critical to verifying the claimed advantages of the approach.
• The *Sprite operating system* was designed to demonstrate several improved techniques for implementing a parallel and distributed operating system, such as the efficiency of new methods of caching and the effectiveness of log-structured file systems.

### Proof of Concept

• *Cosmic cube* was one of the first successful multiprocessor computers using off-the-shelf microprocessors. This machine demonstrated that a range of open problems in building this type of multicomputer were surmountable and that the resulting machines could be used as computational engines in several important scientific problems.
• *Geometry engine* demonstrated that it was possible to use very large scale integration (VLSI) technology to build a much lower cost implementation of what had been very expensive 3-D graphics hardware.
• *Ethernet* demonstrated the feasibility of building a local area network with good performance and low cost.
• *Information hiding* demonstrated improvements in the modularity of programs when the internal structure of those programs was completely concealed from and inaccessible to programmers not responsible for that structure.
• The *cut-copy-paste desktop metaphor* demonstrated its usefulness in thousands of applications for nonprogrammers by drawing close analogies between computer manipulations of information and more familiar scissors-and-tape operations on paper-based text.

### Proof of Existence

• *ALTO* was the first personal computer/workstation to unify several technologies: a bit-mapped screen, a mouse, a local computer, and a local area network. This integrated machine was truly different from computers that had been built before, and it had a profound impact on the development of both workstations and personal computers.
• *Simula* was the first language to introduce the ideas of encapsulation and data abstraction. As such, it created a new set of language features and demonstrated their usefulness. The ideas of Simula have had a profound impact on language design.

programs that translate high-level computer languages into the binary instructions that are executed by computers) often generate redundant instructions, such as loading data into a register when the register already contains those data. This redundancy is the result of the compiler's strategy of translating high-level language statements one at a time. He conjectured that by examining the generated instructions a few at a time (i.e., through a "peephole"), a program optimizer could eliminate many redundancies and thus speed up processing time.

Fraser added an optimizer to an existing compiler and discovered that enormous improvements were possible. Indeed, his optimizer was so successful at removing unnecessary instructions that the time saved in not having to perform other types of processing on those instructions exceeded the time needed to perform the optimizations (i.e., the savings exceeded the cost, and the optimization introduced "negative overhead").

### Proof of Concept

An artifact acting in the proof-of-concept role demonstrates by its behavior that a complex assembly of components can accomplish a particular set of activities, behavior that could not be argued simply by logical reasoning or abstract argument from first principles.

To illustrate by analogy this role in helping ECSE researchers understand complex systems, imagine that frogs did not exist but were being created for the first time. Could a credible case for a frog be made without exhibiting one? The image-processing capability of a frog eye might be describable; the muscle structure of the mouth and tongue, and its actuation by the nervous system, could be comprehensible; and the mechanisms of the nervous system and brain could be explained. Yet using logical argument alone to convince a skeptic (the standard of science) that this collection of mechanisms and processes could catch a passing fly would be inconceivable. The dynamic behavior of this system whose interacting parts can exhibit a multitude of states or configurations is too complex to be defended convincingly by direct analysis. Proof in terms of a demonstration is necessary. The working system, the artifact, is a witness "proving" that the concepts in at least one configuration are correct.

Experimental computers are good examples of proof-of-concept artifacts. A key problem to be solved in parallel computing is how the processors can avoid long delays in accessing or referencing memory. Solutions to this problem have motivated many different computer designs serving proof-of-concept roles. One design uses caches (i.e., small memories local to each processor) and various methods of keeping the caches coherent. A second design uses multithreading (i.e., the ability to execute instructions from several processes simultaneously in order to perform useful work while waiting for memory references to complete). A third design dispenses with hiding memory latency and emphasizes fast interprocess communication. All of these designs focus on memory references, one of the most basic operations of the machine that affects most components of the system. Understanding the effects of different design philosophies from first principles is essentially impossible.

## Proof of Existence

An artifact playing the proof-of-existence role conveys the essence of an entirely new phenomenon. Because computation is synthetic, human creativity can produce phenomena never before imagined, which are often explained better by demonstration than by description.

A very good example of a proof-of-existence artifact is the computer mouse, which is used as a pointing device in human-computer interaction. A verbal description of how a mouse can be used simply does not convey how useful it is as an input device. The mouse was created by Douglas Englebart at SRI International as one of several human-computer communication devices. Although it was described in full technical detail and careful studies were made of its utility,[10] many computer scientists recall first appreciating the significance of the invention not from the published record, but from a film that Englebart produced, showing the mouse in action. The demonstration of the device conveyed the essence of the new phenomenon beyond any amount of description of how or how well it worked.

## Summary

The three roles of artifacts are described above in the order of the frequency with which they are likely to appear in ECSE research: the proof-of-existence role (mentioned last) is rare, and the proof-of-per-

---

[10] The most contemporaneous and complete technical description of the mouse is contained in the following: Engelbart, D.C. 1973. "Design Considerations for Knowledge Workshop Terminals," *AFIPS Conference Proceedings* 42:221-227. It is interesting to compare this paper to a retrospective look at the mouse describing its impact on human-computer interfaces: Engelbart, D.C. 1988. "The Augmented Knowledge Workshop," pp. 185-232 in Adele Goldberg (ed.), *A History of Personal Workstations*. Association of Computing Machinery, New York. This article is also a good resource for those wishing to know what experimentation is like.

formance role (mentioned first) is most common.  As noted, an artifact can act in multiple roles, but perhaps not as frequently as might be expected.  For example, because the peephole optimizer was a first of its kind, it might seem to meet the definition of an artifact serving in the proof-of-concept role, but the actual mechanisms of the optimizer are sufficiently simple (to a practitioner) that its ability to optimize programs would not have been in dispute.  The question was how effective it could be, and that is what Fraser showed.

Other engineering disciplines are also focused on artifacts, and indeed ECSE does share certain characteristics with these other disciplines.  However, the artifacts of other engineering disciplines are typically constrained by well-defined physical phenomena (e.g., gravity, conductance of metals, compressibility of gases).  This limits the variety of the artifacts and presents clear-cut criteria for evaluating their merit.  An aircraft cannot take arbitrary form, and one test for its success is, Does it fly?  By contrast, the synthetic property of ECSE artifacts underconstrains them, as explained below, complicating their creation and evaluation.

## The Artifacts of ECSE Are Extraordinarily Complex

Computing artifacts are often exceedingly complex.  Both the artifact's construction and its dynamic behavior are complicated.  Consequently, creating and understanding artifacts can require considerable intellectual effort.  Complexity of construction takes several forms, including a large number of components and high component specialization.

An illustration of the "many-components" property is the prototype J-machine designed and built by a team at the Massachusetts Institute of Technology.  It contains more than 4,000 chips, more than 1,000 of which are copies of a custom processor chip, designed by the team and requiring 700 pages to specify.  The processor required 1.1 million transistors, and so the resulting computer contained more than 1 billion transistors devoted to active logic, not memory.[11]  Although this project may be less complex than the superconducting super collider or an array telescope, it should be kept in mind that the J-machine is not a mega-project supporting an entire field.  It is the experiment of a single, moderate-size research team—a typical contemporary machine design project, of which there are several ongoing at any time.

---

[11] Dally, William J., et al. 1992. "The Message-Driven Processor: A Multicomputer Processing Node with Efficient Mechanisms," *IEEE Micro* 12(2):23-29.

Software can be at least as complex as hardware, with "modest" prototypes requiring 100,000 lines of code. There are at any given time many more software projects under way than hardware projects, probably because software is the implementation medium of choice for most problems (see discussion of universality below), although it also has lower infrastructure costs. Unlike hardware, which frequently benefits from replication, each line of software is distinct and requires an intellectual action to compose. (For a 100,000-line program, the task of getting the program to work perfectly is roughly analogous to writing a 3,000-page manuscript without a single grammatical, spelling, or plot error.) Also, software development is less advanced than hardware in terms of utilizing standard parts, building blocks, and construction tools, although software development works at higher levels of abstraction.

Complex systems are rarely composed of a multitude of undifferentiated parts, but rather are subdivided into specialized components. These components can often be substantial systems in their own right, requiring extensive specialized knowledge to understand and person-years to create. This "complexity-of-components" property of artifacts is illustrated by database systems, optimizing compilers, and operating systems, but there are many other examples. The core of a typical database design, for example, includes at least five major subsystems: a file manager, a database manager, a query processor, a data manipulation language precompiler, and a data definition language compiler. The subsystems vary in size depending on the sophistication of the design, but their average size is tens of thousands of lines of code. Many other subsystems must be added to this to produce a modern database system. Researchers studying databases routinely create and/or experiment with systems of this magnitude.

A dominant theme in ECSE is reducing complexity by using such strategies as generalization, unification, and abstraction. Indeed, reducing complexity may itself be a creative accomplishment of significance. Yet when the ECSE researcher is successful in reducing complexity, the allure of a more ambitious goal reintroduces additional complexity and complicates the creation of artifacts in a new way.

### ECSE Is Sensitive to Technological Developments

ECSE has an intimate relationship with technology. The technology in which an artifact is implemented is not an incidental aspect of the artifact's construction. Indeed, the availability of a given technology may well determine the feasibility of a good and innovative idea. For example, an application of data compression might fail when the computers that perform the compress/decompress operations are so slow that it would be faster simply to transmit the data uncompressed; however, when computer speeds improve faster than data transmission rates, then the compress-transmit-decompress approach might pay off. In the 1960s, the high cost of individual logic gates made logic gate minimization an important problem in circuit design; the advent of integrated circuits made gates so cheap that minimization became unnecessary. Then in the early 1980s, when chip area was at a premium, area minimization became a hot theoretical topic, only to have the subsequent submicron feature sizes of semiconductors render this a problem of negligible importance.

The use of a cutting-edge technology for a project potentially subjects it to the hazards posed by such technologies (e.g., instability, errors, and delays), whereas using a stable, mature technology carries with it the risk of obsolescence before the project is finished. Reliance on technology is probably obvious for many areas of ECSE, such as hardware and architecture, graphics, and communications. Indeed, it is the advances in technology that often open new research opportunities in ECSE. Examples include small disks and redundant arrays of independent disks, very large scale integration (VLSI) technologies, and reduced instruction set computers (RISCs). Software is critical too, often in the form of CAD tools or other facilities to aid in managing complexity.

Experimental software artifacts require significant software technology infrastructure, although this is not widely appreciated. Such software takes different forms, including developmental tools such as advanced programming languages or "tool kits," subsystems for performing sophisticated kinds of analysis such as dependence analysis or symbolic expression transformers, and standard "parts" such as symbol tables, YACC, and window systems.

Such dependence on technology means that nearly all experimental software systems rely on many components (modules and subsystems) that are peripheral to the specific experiment, with a corresponding increase in system complexity. It is not possible or wise for the experimentalist to create all of this software anew, and yet for the experiment to be "complete" these components are essential. So the ECSE researcher must acquire this peripheral software and build interfaces between it and the rest of the system. The quality of the resulting experiment depends on the availability and quality of this software as much as it relies on the ingenuity of the experimentalist.

The other side to the relationship between ECSE and technology is the fact that in recent years, ECSE research has increasingly been responsible for technological advancement in the computer field. Whereas product development teams for the large computer manufacturers may have been responsible for most of the innovation in the 1960s and 1970s, many widely known computer advancements of the 1980s trace their origins to ECSE research. Examples are known to the average user—RISC processors, networking, window systems, UNIX, relational databases—but many more are hidden inside systems, making them faster, more efficient, or more functional, or they are part of the technological infrastructure that supports the rapid innovation so characteristic of the computer field.

## Computing Artifacts Are Universal

A fifth characteristic of ECSE concerns the fact that computers are malleable and versatile. Unlike other machines, computers are universal, which means that within broad limits, whatever one machine can do, all machines can do. Whereas a washing machine only washes and a coffee grinder only grinds, virtually all computers are capable of word processing, circuit optimization, processing spreadsheets, simulating galaxies, and so on. The speed of the processor, its memory size, or the suitability of its peripheral devices (e.g., its monitor) may make the performance of such tasks impractically slow or cumbersome, but they are possible in principle. Although this property is extremely convenient in many respects, it introduces a serious complication: there is no a priori limit on the functionality of computers, which leads to ever-expanding expectations for the capability of artifacts.

Because there is no reason in principle that the functionality of a previous artifact cannot be incorporated into or used in conjunction with an artifact currently under development, the expectation generally is that it must be. A familiar computing application, document preparation, illustrates this phenomenon, but it occurs widely in more technical situations: the original text editors, which simply allowed the easy creation of files of characters, soon became "word processors" with the addition of sophisticated formatting and laser printing capabilities. Then spell-checking was added, as were the creation and incorporation of graphics. Tools now check for grammatical errors and poor writing style. All of these systems do something that their predecessors did not, such as treating the text as a document with footnotes (formatting), or as English words (spell-checking), or as meaningful English sentences (grammar checkers), or as collections of lines, regions, and planes (graphics). Such demands for increasing functionality result in a steady increase in the complexity of new computer systems, and they stand in sharp contrast to the notion of improved utility, in which a new word processor might simply "do better" that which was done before (e.g., a text editor that makes smaller files of compressed text or allows more sophisticated text substitutions).

There is a second consequence as well. Expectations for increasing functionality can affect other systems that serve similar purposes. For example, spell-checking is a standard feature of most word processors today. This leads to expectations that other systems in which text editing is used (e.g., slide presentation systems) should also incorporate spell-checking. However, because slide presentation systems may use an internal representation of words that is different from that used by word processors, this conceptually simple addition to a slide presentation system may be difficult to implement.

### ECSE Is Not Strongly Coupled to
### Theoretical Computer Science

Experimental computer science and engineering does not depend on an elaborate and formalized theoretical foundation in the same way that, for example, experimental physics can draw on theoretical physics. In physics, the interplay and coupling between experiment and theory are rather tight. Theoretical explanations are found for experimental phenomena and then evaluated on their ability to predict other phenomena. Experiments in physics are designed on the basis of a theory that predicts the phenomena to be observed.

"Theory" in computer science is by tradition very close to mathematics. That is, theoreticians in computer science tend to prove theorems, and the standards for demonstrating correctness are very similar to those traditionally used in mathematics. A good deal of modeling work, which in other engineering disciplines might be considered theoretical in nature, is conducted by experimentalists. In other words, good experimentalists do create models and test (reject or accept) hypotheses, all of which might be considered theoretical work but for accidents of history. However, the complexity of the systems built in ECSE and of the underlying models and theories means that experimental implementation is necessary to evaluate the ideas and the models or theories behind them.

Consequently, an "experiment" in ECSE usually does not verify any prediction from theoretical computer science or rely heavily on a model developed by theoreticians, although as noted above, good experimental work is grounded in testable models and hypotheses. Experiments are most often conducted to validate some informal thesis derived from a computational model that is informed but not rigorously specified by theory and that may have been developed expressly for the experiment. A useful analogy might be that ECSE is today where experimental aeronautical engineering was when most of the information used in the design of airframes came from wind tunnel studies rather than computational fluid dynamics. Although many of the subareas within CS&E are studied theoretically, research in theoretical computer science is coupled to experimental work only in certain specialized topics in which the idealized problem aligns well with the practical problem. For example, language theory underpins the parsing component of compilation, and complexity theory underpins data encryption.

Experimentalists do use theoretical techniques in the conduct of their work. For example, rough estimates of algorithmic complexity are routinely made, and the recognition that a problem is NP-complete directs experimentalists to examine heuristic solutions or redirects the attack toward alternate approaches.[12] These tools are valuable and reinforce the theoretical component in the academic curriculum.

Theoretical work occasionally motivates experimental work. A particularly nice example is Manber's application of techniques from exact string matching algorithms to create extremely fast and powerful approximate string matching software.[13] Although the artifact's new ideas can be cast in theoretical terms, the key accomplishments of the work have been largely experimental—the engineering required to achieve high performance, the experiments on large databases, the performance characteristics of the program, and so on.

Experimental work may motivate theoretical work in CS&E. For example, the first routing protocol used in the Arpanet attempted to use load-sensitive routing based on a distributed routing algorithm. In practice, the algorithm led to oscillatory behavior owing to properties of the protocol, the method used for measuring load, and the selection of parameters. In retrospect, computer scientists were able to explain theoretically the reasons for the oscillations, but it was implementation and experimentation that led them to identify and address the question. The complexity of computational systems makes

---

[12] An NP-complete problem is one that takes a very long time to solve as a function of input size. More specifically, so-called computationally tractable problems can be solved in "polynomial time" (i.e., in a time that increases as a function of input size no faster than some power of the input size). NP-complete problems are believed to be computationally intractable (i.e., the solution of an NP-complete problem is believed to require a time that increases more rapidly than polynomially).

[13] Wu, S., and U. Manber. 1992. "Fast Text Searching Allowing Errors," *Communications of the ACM* 35(10):83-91.

experimentation critical, because it is often infeasible to anticipate all the important interactions and behaviors.

Overall, ECSE is not tightly coupled to, or heavily reliant on, theoretical computer science, although the two intermingle at points along their boundary. Experimental exploration is crucial to understanding the terrain of the field and seems to be a precondition to building permanent foundations.

One conclusion to draw is that contrary to a widely held assumption (within the field[14] as well as outside it), physics is not a good model for the relationship between experimentation and theory in CS&E. The fact that experimentation and theory are today largely independent areas with little interplay introduces the possibility that a computer science or engineering faculty member might not be well acquainted with research methodologies in the "other" specialty.[15] That possibility raises serious concerns about how professional accomplishments are to be evaluated for the purposes of promotion (see Chapter 4).

## A Succinct Definition of Experimental Computer Science and Engineering

With the foregoing background, a succinct definition of ECSE can be formulated: *ECSE involves the creation of, or the experimentation with or on, computational artifacts. Artifacts,* which are implementations of one or more computational phenomena, generally take the form of hardware or software systems, but the term should be broadly construed. Artifacts are usually complex in terms of both the number and the integration of components, and their creation often requires considerable intellectual effort. An artifact can be the subject of a study, the apparatus for the study, or both. ECSE, being in its early exploratory stage, is not well supported by theory; therefore, *experimentation* carries different connotations in ECSE than it has in physics, biology, or medicine.

---

[14] One would imagine that this point is known at least to computer science faculty, but in the testimony received by the committee it was asserted by a departmental chair that "experimentalists are verifying the predictions of the theory of PRAMs—parallel random access machines." They are not. Indeed, no experiment has been proposed. Because most theorems about PRAMs assert properties of asymptotic behavior, it is unclear what prediction a finite set of experiments could confirm.

[15] Not incidentally, this fact also explains how some departments of computer science can have thriving intellectual programs without a significant representation of experimentalists.

## MORE ON ARTIFACTS

Artifacts and the computational phenomena they embody are fundamental to CS&E. Yet perhaps because they have only recently (since World War II) become the subject of academic study and because they are not well treated in terms of their scientific content in secondary schools, college science "literacy" classes, or the popular scientific press, artifacts may not be as widely understood as, say, biological phenomena. This section elaborates further on artifacts and their roles in ECSE.

Artifacts often have an "all-or-nothing" quality to them: either all of the components are functioning, and the device works and is suitable for experimentation, or one or more of the components are not working, and the device cannot be used. Examples include computers, robots, operating system kernels, and the like. Most highly integrated artifacts do not run until they are essentially complete. This all-or-nothing property does not concern the question of whether the working parts have "bugs," nor does it concern the "add-on" components that many artifacts require to be complete. Rather, it concerns the fact that in highly integrated systems the basic "operating cycle" may rely on a large number of components. An analogy would be an aircraft: before a test flight, the airframe and all of the power and control elements must be operational, although the galley need not be.

Because computation is synthetic, human creativity can produce phenomena never before imagined; such phenomena are often explained better by demonstration than by description. Early computers themselves (e.g., Anatasoff's machine and ENIAC[16]) were proofs of existence. Yet much of what is embodied in the proof-of-existence role concerns conveying intangibles. Much of the significance of the mouse or animated graphic images is knowable only through nonverbal channels. It is virtually impossible to write about such intangibles, and so knowledge about them is not easily archived.

Computer graphics is a research area that relies heavily on artifacts to convey intangibles. The channel is visual perception, of course. In instances where the subject concerns a single image, the artifact, namely a program on a graphic workstation, creates a still picture. However, for dynamic images, an artifact—either the program running on a graphic workstation or a film of the image sequence—is

---

[16] These were among the first computers developed in the early days of electronic computing.

essential to illustrating what has been accomplished. It is obvious, for example, that the demonstration of a flight simulator can convey information beyond that provided in a paper about the simulator. Seeing the image develop in time is simply more powerful, more convincing, and more inclusive than describing what it would look like.[17] Another instance from the world of graphics would be more "natural" light reflectance in a graphic image. Notice that the "intangible" need not always concern matters of perception. Because "better" could be a matter of personal taste, reasonable observers could disagree on whether this use of a proof-of-existence artifact is a contribution or not.

Proof-of-concept artifacts can sometimes be employed to illustrate the creation of hardware or software using a new methodology. An example is the classic work of Parnas on information hiding.[18] Here, the artifact is used chiefly to exhibit the properties claimed for the methodology. A human uses the methodology to produce an artifact, and the artifact is assessed. In CAD systems, where an artifact assists in the production of other artifacts, the methodology may be carried out by a combination of human and computer activity. Synthesis systems that produce circuit layouts for silicon chips are an example. The challenge with this use of artifacts often is determining the proper metrics with which to assess the artifact from which inferences can be drawn about the methodology.

Simulation is a powerful methodology, and ECSE researchers use simulation extensively. Occasionally it is asked, Why create the artifact at all? Why not simply simulate it? Such questions often apply to computers and chips, both of which are expensive to build physically. Generally, the answer is that the simulator must account for the behavior of so many parts that a simulated artifact runs much more slowly than a real artifact would: an instruction-level simulation of a computer may run 1,000 times more slowly than the computer itself, and chips can require hours to simulate a few nanoseconds of activity. Thus, creating the artifact is essential to getting any quantity of experience with it. Usually, in the first few seconds that these hardware artifacts run they exhibit more behavior than during the months of simulation used in their design.

---

[17] For example, computer simulations of airplanes in flight are used to train pilots to fly real aircraft, but mere verbal descriptions of how to fly airplanes would clearly not suffice.

[18] Parnas, David. 1972. "On the Criteria to Be Used in Decomposing Systems into Modules," *Communications of the ACM* 5(12):1053-1058.

The performance of artifacts serving a proof-of-performance role is measured in order to understand how well they perform, but the precise numerical values that result from such measurement are rarely "constants" in the same way that the melting point of zinc is a constant. The reason is that different artifacts serving the same function can be expected to have different performance characteristics. For example, had Fraser used a different compiler or a different suite of test programs, his numbers would have been different, because different host compilers will generate code with different redundancy characteristics, and different programs will be optimized by different amounts. Nor is the relative property of "negative overhead" an outcome that must necessarily occur in any reproduction of Fraser's experiment, although this could indeed be the case. The significance of his measurements was, among other things, that they quantified for compiler writers the effectiveness of limited-context optimizations, showing such things as sensitivity to peephole size or optimization type.

## COMPARISONS WITH OTHER FIELDS

Experimental computer science and engineering shares much with other fields of engineering. Engineering disciplines are ultimately concerned with the creation of artifacts (e.g., computer systems, airplanes, power plants, and automobiles) that provide significant practical utility and functionality for human users. A considerable amount of engineering research is devoted to improving artifacts; thus, aerospace engineers try to build better planes, civil engineers try to build better roads, and experimental computer scientists and engineers try to build better computing systems.

However, despite the importance of the end user, a great deal of engineering research is devoted to improving these artifacts in ways that are not necessarily obvious to the end user (e.g., the artifact is made easier to manufacture). Economics matters to engineering, because artifacts that are useful to human beings must also be affordable and practical to construct. Thus, one type of achievement in any engineering discipline is the design of an artifact that consumes significantly fewer resources to provide the same functionality as its predecessor.

In all of these cases, then, engineers try to create better artifacts (i.e., artifacts that offer greater utility or functionality in the computational setting, or the same utility for a smaller investment of resources). Because what is better is at root a human judgment, engineering—in ECSE as in other fields—often involves a degree of creativity and insight into how an artifact can be made better.

ECSE also has marked similarities to other specific fields. Most obviously, ECSE shares the synthetic property with other parts of CS&E and with other fields such as mathematics. The universality of computers influences research in theoretical computer science, although in quite a different way than it does in ECSE.

Yet there are similarities in other dimensions as well. For example, materials science and biotechnology are technical disciplines that share with ECSE a close coupling with a rapidly changing technology. This is not to say that other areas of science and engineering do not profit from advances in technology. They clearly do. However, the advances at the frontiers of the discipline are not tied so closely to technology on a day-to-day basis as they are in these fields.

An important difference between ECSE and other engineering disciplines is the previously discussed difference between "functionality" and "utility." Experimental computer scientists and engineers are subject to the demands for ever-increasing functionality. By contrast, an aircraft designer strives for greater utility through improved fuel economy, greater safety, quieter operation, and so on, but greater functionality is never at issue. An airplane carries passengers through the air. It need not, for example, navigate through city traffic—a task reserved for taxis because of obvious physical constraints. Although the distinction between greater functionality and greater utility may be a matter of degree rather than one of kind (indeed, flying cars have been built), designers of computing artifacts nearly always have greater functionality as a design option, principally because no physical constraints prevent it.

## WHY UNIVERSITIES SHOULD PERFORM ECSE RESEARCH

Because industrial products grow quite naturally out of the artifacts of ECSE, it could be asked, Why shouldn't ECSE be the exclusive province of industry? The committee has identified several reasons to conduct ECSE research in universities.

Perhaps the most significant reason to conduct ECSE research at universities is to ensure adequate intellectual diversity. For 10 technical concepts to reach maturity and be injected into the technology base, "a thousand flowers must bloom." As explained above, it is difficult to predict how well processes, algorithms, and mechanisms work in practice and how well they work together. Artifacts must be built to understand their behavior. Of these research prototype systems, perhaps only 1 in 10 is worthy of advanced development. Of the advanced development systems, perhaps only 1 in 10 is worthy of product development and production. The numbers are not exact, of course, but rather are intended to suggest how commercial benefits result from the fittest survivors in a diverse environment of technical competition. A concept survives when its technical merit justifies the increased costs of the next level of development, perhaps a factor of 10 greater than the previous level. Although few research artifacts become products, far more of them influence the research community, and ideas from them become incorporated in some way in subsequent research.

If performing experimental research at universities adds diversity, expanding the number of universities doing experimental research in CS&E further enriches the intellectual environment. The theory community in computer science is strengthened by a diversity of participants, and a glance at any list of participants at the conference on Foundations of Computer Science and the Symposium on the Theory of Computing will reveal a wide variety of institutional homes for those participants. Although it may be unrealistic to expect a comparable diversity in ECSE (because of the infrastructure and resource constraints discussed in Chapter 2), it would be clearly undesirable for only a few academic institutions to perform ECSE research. Individual institutions develop their own research styles and foci, and if the institutions doing such research are too few, important avenues of investigation may be overlooked. Many universities have become more competitive in ECSE research over the past dozen years through programs such as the NSF's Coordinated Experimental Research program, the Defense Department's University Research Instrumentation program, and corporate equipment donations. The success of these programs demonstrates that direct intervention can expand the number of competitive schools.

An additional reason for performing ECSE research in the university environment is the enrichment it gives to the educational mission. Faculty engaged in research keep the curriculum fresh and vitalize the content of design courses. They can and must offer graduate students advanced seminars in their research area, which prepares some to conduct research on the topic and educates others. For lower-level classes, it is frequently possible to select examples from problems encountered in research that can enliven the topic for both students and teacher. However, the most valuable benefit may be that conducting research keeps a faculty member current. Given its strong connections to technology, CS&E evolves rapidly, and a degree program can quickly become antiquated and obsolete without continual refreshment.

Still another reason is that as a discipline, CS&E has close ties to industry. The majority of undergraduate computer science majors find employment in industry; about half of the new Ph.D.s in CS&E do so as well.[19] Without exposure to ECSE in their formal education, students would be even less prepared than they are now to engage in meaningful careers in industry. As an associate professor at a large private university noted in response to the CRA-CSTB survey (see Appendix A):

> The practical aspects of compiler optimization are passed on verbally or in the occasional "engineering oriented" compiler text, while texts that focus on different grammars and parsing algorithms are considered to be more "pure." Likewise, practical software testing methodologies are often given far less discussion than impractical but theoretically elegant methods. In architecture texts, issues such as signal delays, noise, loading, power, and cost usually take a back seat to the intellectually important issues of organization, instruction sets, and theoretical or simulated performance analysis. This bias is a contributing factor to the common complaint among industrial employers that graduates have to be retrained because they have no practical experience. Obviously, academe cannot and should not recast itself into a training ground for industrial employers, but an increased amount of practical and genuine experimentation would be a benefit to the discipline.

Finally, a strong experimental component to the research and teaching programs of CS&E departments is a necessary aspect of reaching out to other academic disciplines. As articulated in *Computing the Future*, the future of the discipline demands in part an attention to problems with relevance to society or to other intellectual domains.

None of this argues that universities and industrial research laboratories are equivalent research environments. Industrial laboratories such as those at AT&T Bell Laboratories generally have better resources and fewer distractions, and their efforts are funded by their parent corporations specifically in the hope and expectation that they will lead to competitive advantages in the marketplace. Sometimes they offer unique advantages, such as proprietary technology or access to profiles of (the parent company's) customers' work loads. Universities offer different advantages, including the enthusiasm and imagination of graduate students and a wide freedom to select topics for study. Despite these differences, both settings have produced important experimental research ideas in recent years.

---

[19]Gries, David, and Dorothy Marsh. 1992. "The 1990-1991 Taulbee Survey," *Computing Research News* 4 (January):8.

# 2
# An Academic Career in ECSE

William Blake's dream "to see the world in a grain of sand" almost becomes reality for those choosing a career in experimental computer science and engineering (ECSE). Building ever more amazing machines out of silicon and alternate worlds in software challenges the intellect and rewards creativity. Although the academic setting provides enormous intellectual freedom to choose problems and the independence to follow one's curiosity, an academic career in ECSE demands not so much the traits of a dreamer as it does the skills of the entrepreneur. One must organize implementation efforts, formulate goals, build a team, find funding (Box 2.1), and more, as well as handle the traditional academic demands that entrepreneurs do not have, such as teaching, directing dissertations, staying abreast of the literature, and serving on deans' committees. Successful experimentalists not only dream the future; they also implement it.

In this chapter an academic career in ECSE is characterized from the research point of view. The chapter begins with a discussion of the goals of ECSE research and proceeds to consider the infrastructure and support requirements for achieving those goals.

## GOALS OF RESEARCH IN ECSE

The purpose of research is to contribute to the knowledge base of the field. In the natural sciences, creating something new (e.g., lawrencium

---

**BOX 2.1  Ideas Require Technology, Funding, and Management**

Had it been built, the analytical engine of Charles Babbage would have been the first general-purpose computing machine, although, belonging to the mid-1800s, it would have been implemented mechanically rather than electronically. For many years, historians of computing have believed that the analytical engine was never built because the engineering techniques of the time could not support its construction (perhaps due to insufficiently precise manufacturing tolerances). In this view, the first general-purpose computing machine had to wait until the advent of electronic technology.

Recent evidence suggests that this view is inaccurate. Indeed, in 1991, a working model of the analytical engine was built, using only parts that could have been manufactured in the 1840s. The engineers responsible for building this working model argue that Babbage was unable to build the analytical engine not because of a lack of an appropriate implementing technology, but because of his inability to keep costs under control.

SOURCE: Swade, Doron. 1993. "Redeeming Charles Babbage's Mechanical Computer," *Scientific American* 261(February):86-91.

---

or rubella vaccine) is unquestionably a contribution, because of the constraints imposed by the physical world and the creation's relationship to other physical phenomena. In a synthetic discipline such as ECSE, however, where it is straightforward to create something new, novelty is not enough to establish a contribution. Frederick Brooks of the University of North Carolina points out that the evaluation of scholarly work in synthetic fields is subject to an obligation that is not characteristic in natural fields. In particular, he observes that:

> When one discovers a fact about nature, it is a contribution per se no matter how small. Since anyone can create something new [in a synthetic field], that alone does not establish a contribution. Rather one must show that the creation is better.[1]

This task—establishing that a creation is better and a contribution has been made—is intimately connected with the artifact in ECSE.

---

[1] Personal communication to the committee, October 1992.

Subdisciplines of computer science such as theoretical computer science and, to some extent, computational mathematics establish that a contribution has been made by using criteria that are also employed in mathematics. For example, a complexity bound is "better" if it is tighter, and a theorem solving a long-standing open question is prima facie a contribution. Intangibles such as "elegance," "depth," and "mathematical sophistication" also figure into the evaluation. The key question in these subdisciplines is, Has the proposition been proved? Moreover, there is often considerable consensus that a given theoretical result is or is not new, although theoreticians may disagree over its importance or significance.

In ECSE, computational concepts and phenomena are judged to be better through studying and measuring the artifacts that implement them. Thus, the artifact can be the subject of the study, the apparatus for the study, or both. Relevant questions are, Is the implementation faster or more efficient in other ways? Does the idea provide greater functionality? and, Does the idea materially improve the process of creating artifacts? The criteria for recognizing when a contribution has been made depend first on whether the artifact is acting in a proof-of-performance, proof-of-concept, or proof-of-existence role.

In a proof-of-performance role, the artifact is usually the apparatus, and better can mean more efficient. Efficiency metrics include higher speed, smaller memory requirements, less frequent disk references, and so on. Better in this sense is determined by direct measurement and is quantitative. When Fraser's peephole optimizer saved more in linkage editing time than it cost in added code generation time, quantities that were measured in seconds, the optimizer was self-evidently better.

In the proof-of-performance context, better can also mean more functional. Enhanced functionality is interpreted broadly and includes being more expressive, as in programming languages; having a larger vocabulary, as in a speech understanding system; and being more robust to errors, as in data transmission or storage systems. A common form of "more functional" is having greater generality, either in terms of admitting more cases or removing assumptions about operating context. Interestingly, it is even possible to be better by being less general, if doing so can be argued not to be significantly restrictive and there is an opportunity for greater efficiency in some other dimension. An example would be relaxing strict memory consistency to allow shared memory multiprocessors greater latitude in hiding memory latency.

For artifacts whose behavior is not well understood, some proof-of-performance research seeks to understand specific properties of their behavior.   In such cases, the experimentalist investigates an artifact produced by someone else.   In contrast to the instances above, in which the purpose of experimentation is often to demonstrate the superiority of the experimental artifact over some other artifact, the value of the experimental artifact is accepted as a premise and the research goal is to understand specific properties of it.   For example, networks are ubiquitous and their value is indisputable, but careful study of the behavior of different networks (e.g., load-balancing on the Arpanet or the fairness of Ethernet's exponential back-off protocol) is essential to understanding networking.   In these cases, research may demonstrate that one or another implementation of a concept may be better under particular sets of circumstances.

In a proof-of-concept role, an artifact is usually the subject of the research.   In many of these cases, the dimensions along which a given artifact may be better may be heavily weighted toward the intangible.   For example, better may mean "makes a programmer more productive," which must be determined by use.   Utility can be difficult to establish, because the value of a new capability in computing is not always evident.   For the natural frog, catching a fly is obviously beneficial.   Would it be useful to build a robotic frog for catching a fly?   Similarly, how is a new programming methodology or a new system for computer-assisted chip design more useful?

The computer-aided design (CAD) tool research of John Ousterhout illustrates how such evaluations are often accomplished.   His work on Caesar[2] provided a graphic capability for chip design that did not exist previously.   Ousterhout did not run experiments comparing the old design approach to Caesar, measuring for a suite of circuits the design time, number of errors, and so on.[3]   Instead, he distributed the software, and designers voted for the system, and its successor Magic,[4] by obtaining a copy and using it.   Their voluntary use of it proved beyond any number of controlled studies that the system was better.   For such reasons, when—in ECSE—better means more useful, the number of users may well be evidence of impact.

---

[2] Ousterhout, J. 1984. "The User Interface and Implementation of an IC Layout Editor," *IEEE Transactions on Computer Aided Design* 3(3):242-249.

[3] There are numerous problems with conducting such comparative studies because the tool is used to create artifacts, and it is usually impossible to decide what properties of an artifact have been influenced by use of the tool or what the figures of merit should be for determining quality.

[4] Ousterhout, J., G. Hamachi, G. Mayo, W. Scott, and G.S. Taylor. 1985. "The Magic VLSI Layout System," *IEEE Design and Test of Computers* 2(1):19-30.

In a proof-of-existence role, artifacts are often obviously better because they provide a never-before-thought-of capability. Indeed, the idea may be so useful that it is quickly absorbed into the consciousness of the field, and explicit credit for the contribution is no longer given. The principal issue in determining whether a proof-of-existence artifact is a contribution concerns how quickly its worth is recognized. By definition, these artifacts offer a never-before-thought-of capability, which may be "ahead of its time." It may take a while for the community to appreciate the concept fully.

In addition to improving hardware and software, much of the field is concerned with the technology of producing hardware and software more efficiently. This motivates research into CAD tools and more expressive programming languages. What is better is determined indirectly in these cases (i.e., the artifact is evaluated to infer information about the efficacy of the tool or method used to produce it). One challenge for experimentalists is to find the proper metrics for artifacts that will imply useful information about those tools or methods.

Experimental projects—especially large ones—often commingle old and new ideas. Thus, in some cases the true contribution may not be so much the presence of new ideas per se, but rather a novel synthesis of ideas, whether new or old. The UNIX operating system is a case in point. Many of its features (e.g., support for time-sharing, hierarchical file systems, pipes for routing input/output) had been implemented in previous systems; nevertheless, UNIX was a major contribution to ECSE because of its simplicity and ease of modification and use.

Finally, consider the question, Under what circumstances can implementation be considered research? It should be obvious that creating a computational artifact, be it a program, digital hardware, graphic image, or the like, is not synonymous with conducting experimental computer science research. ECSE researchers often program, but programming (even programming of a system that has never before been written[5]) is not necessarily ECSE research.

Constructing an artifact is research when it contributes directly or indirectly to our understanding of computing. This general formulation implies two specific requirements:

---

[5] For example, programmers at software development houses routinely write programs that have never before been written, so that in this sense these programs are new. But they are not implementing new concepts or demonstrating new computational phenomena.

1. The artifact must embody some computational phenomenon in a manner that reveals new information. Thus the artifact will serve in one of the standard roles, or a similar capacity, and it must be constructed in a way that conveys the information reliably (i.e., it is stable and methodologically sound).

2. The new information is extracted from the artifact and conveyed in a suitable medium and scholarly manner. If the person constructing the artifact is the *only* person obtaining new and useful information from it, it is not research. Rather, to be research the implementor must teach *others*. The research community must learn of the discovery in a way that connects it to the existing knowledge base.

Thus, clear exposition and explanation of innovations are as critical to research as having new ideas or even building a new artifact. A good example is provided by Richard Stallman's EMACS editor. This work made use of concepts that had been known previously—dynamic binding and dynamic loading—but it was not until Stallman explained and demonstrated their significance in the editing context that these concepts became widely applied in this setting.

The above questions have little to do with whether or not the researcher has a particular application in mind when he or she undertakes the research. Put differently, the traditional distinction between "basic" and "applied" research does not hold up under close examination.[6] However, efforts devoted solely to making an innovative artifact usable by others not in the research team (e.g., writing documentation) do not constitute research in any sense of the word, although such efforts may be indispensable if an artifact is to be disseminated widely and its contribution evaluated.

## RESOURCES FOR ECSE RESEARCH

### Equipment and Software

The creation of, or experimentation with, computational artifacts requires equipment. It follows, therefore, that infrastructure resources—equipment and related support facilities—are not optional for an academic research career in ECSE.

---

[6] For more discussion of this point, see Computer Science and Telecommunications Board. 1992. *Computing the Future.* National Academy Press, Washington, D.C.

In the CRA-CSTB survey of ECSE graduate students (described in Appendix A), a substantial majority of respondents cited lack of adequate infrastructure as the primary drawback for them in seeking or taking an academic position. Similarly, a majority of students who preferred industry jobs cited a better infrastructure for research as an important reason for their preference.

Experimental computer science and engineering research requires hardware, software, or both. The following subsections describe some of the difficulties related to building and maintaining adequate equipment and software facilities at the research frontier.[7]

### Staying on the Cutting Edge in Equipment

Equipment is essential to any laboratory science. However, laboratory equipment for ECSE has an extraordinarily short lifetime at the cutting edge; in a National Science Foundation (NSF) survey conducted in 1985-1986, administrators from computer science departments regarded research instrumentation and equipment that was more than one year old (on average) as not "state of the art."[8] Over the years, advances in the hardware state of the art have been truly dramatic, improving by factors of more than 100 in speed and memory capacity in the last decade. This exceeds the speed improvement in aircraft between the Wright brothers' airplane and the SR-71. At the same time, there have been dramatic reductions in hardware cost. It is possible to conduct some meaningful experimental research without having equipment that is on the absolute cutting edge, but with rates of improvement this dramatic, equipment quickly becomes antiquated to a degree that affects research.

Software is generally as important as hardware. The base computing environment for ECSE is the UNIX operating system, for which an enormous amount of software is available. Tools from UNIX, such as Lex and YACC, are widely used building blocks and so standard as not to occasion explicit mention by most researchers in enumerating their software needs. Examples of less ubiquitous, but nevertheless widely used, software include CAD tools for chip design,

---

[7] While the committee is most familiar with the demands of ECSE, it does not wish to claim that the field's requirements for resources are necessarily greater than those of other fields with defining characteristics similar to those used to describe ECSE in Chapter 1. Such fields include, for example, biotechnology and materials science.

[8] See National Science Foundation. 1988. *Academic Research Equipment in Selected Science/Engineering Fields: 1982-1983 to 1985-1986.* SRS 88-D1. NSF, Washington, D.C., Table B-5, p. B-14.

specialized language translators (e.g., Common Lisp) that support prototyping and symbolic computation, building blocks such as Interviews and the synthesizer generator, dozens of simulators for computer systems, and so on. To this list can be added specific tools and systems specialized for a particular research area, which are typically exchanged gratis and unsupported.

### Dedicated Computing Systems

Experimental software research often requires dedicated systems (and, on occasion, special-purpose systems) and cannot use the general-purpose computing environment that already exists in the department, school, or university. Much experimental work (e.g., in network and operating systems work and, in some cases, databases) cannot be conducted on shared resources (e.g., campus computing facilities, teaching facilities, or department-wide resources).

The reason is that experimental software is more than just an application running on top of an operating system; the experimental software may *be* the operating system, communications, and/or data storage system itself. In a general-purpose computing environment, these components are vital to all users and so must run flawlessly. Users (rather than researchers) who simply want a computing task performed without regard for how it is performed may be harmed.

For example, researchers who are evaluating a new mechanism for managing the storage of data on large disk arrays will probably construct a functional prototype, test it under controlled conditions to see if it exhibits good performance, and characterize the trade-offs between various design choices. Only then will they attempt to debug the system fully so that it operates well under the wide range of conditions that a general-purpose system experiences. While the system is in the exploratory stages, the development and debugging process would not be tolerated by other users of the system because it would disrupt their ability to carry out their computing work. Computing is central to many research, teaching, and administrative activities. Consequently, the university's or department's general computing facilities (e.g., computing center) are not a realistic option for supporting experimental work. Similarly, non-ECSE users cannot risk using experimental systems.

### Specialized Systems

Experimental hardware systems research requires access to hardware production and testing facilities or services. In some fields such as computer vision and robotics, a researcher needs special-purpose interfaces to cameras and other devices. Even if the hardware can be bought without constructing special-purpose interface hardware, it still requires modifications of the operating system software (e.g., special device drivers) in order to be incorporated into the desired experimental system. In other computationally intensive fields such as graphics, computing power and speed assume the utmost importance, and the necessary power and speed are rarely delivered by off-the-shelf hardware. In still other fields (e.g., VLSI design), the proof of a chip design is the actual fabrication and demonstration of the chip; simulations, although helpful, do not constitute the final proof. Although the Advanced Research Projects Agency (ARPA) provides to academic researchers a Metal-Oxide Semiconductor Implementation Service (MOSIS) and access to (shared) foundry facilities, thus solving the problem of fabricating the chip, considerable equipment is needed to design and test the chip.

### Space

The above-mentioned special needs for equipment lead to the often equally problematic need for space, both for the equipment itself and for the students and staff involved in developing and maintaining it. However, CS&E departments have traditionally found space in short supply. In some instances, this is simply a consequence of the rapid growth of the field, and in other cases it is the result of historical accident, in which computer science departments growing out of mathematics had no laboratory tradition.

Project-specific laboratory space is essential: it provides a location for shared laboratory equipment, a site for constructing physical artifacts, and the meeting site or "community" where the corporate knowledge of the implementation effort is disseminated. General-access laboratories (e.g., terminal rooms) do not generally suffice for these purposes, nor does the alternative suggested for software projects of placing a workstation on individual graduate students' desks. Moreover, in many cases the space must be contiguous to be used effectively, because it is difficult to maintain control over, and run experiments on, equipment that is dispersed throughout a department or building. For this reason, ECSE research is similar to research in chemistry or physics in its need for dedicated laboratory space.

A final complication is that laboratory space must be specially equipped with power and air-conditioning capacity that is not found in standard office or teaching space. Although less expensive than a wet laboratory or facilities suitable for laboratory animals, ECSE laboratory space often involves significant institutional impediments because of the widespread space crunch found in most engineering schools, if not universities in general. It is rare to find currently unused space, and even if one does, it often is unusable as a laboratory without a significant investment in upgrading power and air conditioning.

Providing such space and perhaps other auxiliary services for equipment may provide an additional advantage with respect to fundraising: such facilities and services are often regarded as significant evidence of a department's or university's commitment to a research project by potential industry or government sponsors who may fund equipment grants or donations.

## Maintaining the Research Environment

A research laboratory requires more than state-of-the-art workstations and air conditioning to be a productive environment. Keeping it current requires such common activities as installing and configuring workstations, hardware maintenance at the board-swap level, installing software, upgrading software, interfacing locally produced artifacts with standard facilities, preparing locally produced software for distribution, and so on. None of these is a research activity, but they are all essential to research productivity. Two special cases are hardware and software maintenance.

Equipment is not useful, at least not for very long, without maintenance support. The cost of hardware maintenance alone can equal that of the hardware itself over the lifetime of the equipment. This is particularly true for facilities that are too small to experience economies of scale. Although simple maintenance (e.g., replacing one circuit board with another) can be performed by laboratory members, special contracts are usually needed to ensure continued operation of special-purpose or large-scale machines (e.g., parallel computers).

Perhaps the most time-consuming and least understood laboratory maintenance task is to propagate software changes: often when one system is improved, systems that use it must be changed to take advantage of the improvements or to accommodate revisions in representation. For example, when a windows package is revised, systems using the package may have to be revised to provide access to the new facilities. When staff are not available to perform these functions, the duties fall to the research staff, the faculty, and graduate students. Because these tasks are time-consuming, they diminish the available research time substantially.

## Graduate Students

Graduate students, although they occasionally disparage their role as "slave labor," are in fact critical to experimental research, as they are for work in other fields. In ECSE, they are the highly skilled creators of new artifacts. Artifacts are extremely labor intensive to construct, and although every faculty experimentalist would happily return to the laboratory to work on and experiment with the artifacts, there simply is not enough time in a professor's day. (This is an oft-heard lament of academic experimentalists.)

Construction of artifacts is labor-intensive not only because they are large and complex, involving a great deal of low-level detail, but also because many artifacts are ill-specified when first created and so require technically sophisticated builders capable of working from concepts rather than detailed blueprints. Representations must be created; algorithms must be invented. Moreover, it is often the case that the artifact under study is incorporated into another, existing artifact. Because the two systems will essentially never be "plug-to-plug compatible" with each other, the host system will have to be understood. Development of such understanding often requires a substantial intellectual effort unrelated to a better understanding of the artifact under study, although such effort occasionally has educational value.

Because graduate students are creating artifacts from concepts, they must have suitable background, skills, and knowledge to be successful. Further, as a result of having spent time in the laboratory, studying, building, and experimenting with artifacts, graduate students not only acquire important technical information about their research area, but also learn experimental methodologies. Such practical experience is essential to becoming a successful experimentalist.

## Staff Support

Although graduate students are an important component of infrastructure without which ECSE faculty cannot be productive, many experimental systems projects reach a point at which it is difficult to make progress on the basis of graduate student labor alone. When such a point is reached, technical support staff (including technicians and other paraprofessionals) are necessary to assist with laboratory maintenance and implementation.

Even when only a single technical staff member is available, staff can play a significant role in ensuring that the laboratory remains a productive place to work. Keeping the software current is extremely important. Also, there are significant portions of most implementation efforts that, although essential to the success of the project, are usually peripheral to the main subject of the research. Examples for a compiler project might be linking and loading routines, library routines, interfacing to vendor input/output packages, and so on. Staff members can contribute importantly to the success of a project by implementing these more standardized components.

When technical support staff are available, graduate students are freed to focus more time on the interesting parts of the development with greater "research value" and less on the more routine or lower-level (although necessary) components of the system building. Support staff also provide more continuity in implementation because they are not subject to the vagaries of student course load, attrition, studying for qualifying examinations, and so on. Finally, they often have greater low-level system expertise than do graduate students. (In a recent NSF workshop, Research in Experimental Computer Science,[9] it was noted also that technical support staff have learned to value the simplicity of a system.)

For large ECSE projects, a considerable degree of administrative support is also necessary. Such support coordinates and manages communications and information flow between collaborators, between the research team and other institutions, and among vendors, technicians, and the research team itself.

### Access to Collaborators and Other Experimental Systems

Although faculty collaborators are not essential to all experimental research, and a single investigator with graduate students may be sufficient for many projects, especially those of modest scale, larger-scale systems research is rarely done in isolation; junior faculty members undertaking large-scale systems research are poorly served when they are advised to refrain from collaboration. A good project builds on the work of others for reasons related to productivity, evaluation, dissemination, and impact.

In particular, by collaborating or building on the work of others, an individual researcher can have more impact than by working alone and/or starting from scratch. As an associate professor at a major private university noted in response to the CRA-CSTB survey:

---

[9] Liskov, Barbara. 1992. *Report on Workshop on Research in Experimental Computer Science*. MIT/LCS/TR-540. Laboratory for Computer Science, Massachusetts Institute of Technology, Cambridge, p. 23.

Today, many tools are publicly available (with source code). To avoid the long start-up penalty usually encountered in experimental work, start with one of these systems—like the Gnu compilers or Fraser's lcc system. While they won't necessarily do things the way you think they should be done, they will allow you to begin working, publishing, and refining your intuitions. You can implement your own system from scratch later.

Faculty can save valuable time and resources by using public domain and even commercial system components, even though such use may result in an increased dependence on access to the most current research (and sometimes commercial) software and hardware components and the people that create them.

Another motivation for building on the work of others is related to evaluation. A researcher who develops systems completely unfamiliar to other researchers is at a considerable disadvantage, because these other researchers will find it more difficult to provide meaningful feedback. As a full professor at a major public university put it, "Work on common architectures, systems, and languages so other researchers will be interested in using your prototypes."

In order to evaluate whether a technical innovation is "good," or to quantify "how good" it is in relation to other approaches, a researcher must demonstrate how the new mechanism compares in supporting the range of intended functions. Daily use of an innovation by collaborators is frequently a good way to obtain feedback on its advantages and disadvantages, especially as word of the innovation is disseminated beyond the local user community.

Finally, collaboration is essential for large system-building efforts because the subsystems of an artifact are often so specialized that expertise beyond that of a single researcher is needed. A typical parallel computer research project—including hardware designers, architects, operating systems, programming languages, and applications personnel—requires diverse skills. The Internet itself emerged from a collaboration (at times formal and at other times informal) of perhaps 150 researchers both in the United States and abroad. Common Lisp, a computer language for artificial intelligence, was the result of collaborative efforts among more than 60 researchers in industry, government, and academia.[10]

If a researcher is not at one of a very few universities that have large-scale, multiinvestigator projects, another way of contributing to

---

[10] Computer Science and Telecommunications Board. 1993. *National Collaboratories: Applying Information Technology for Scientific Research*. National Academy Press, Washington, D.C., p. 9.

a development that will have significant impact is to join a group of people working on a common problem.[11]   Consequently, working with colleagues is a matter not only of getting access to results and artifacts quickly, but also of being a part of a collaborative effort. Yet collaboration is not just a matter of sharing words and a white board; one must be "tied in" enough to share development environment, tools, and sometimes equipment. Young faculty starting careers at institutions where they do not have colleagues need to rely on advisers and mentors to help establish and solidify these connections.

## Funding

All of the infrastructure components referred to so far—equipment, graduate students, staff, and even access to collaborators and to experimental and commercial software—require money. By and large, these are expenses that are not incurred in as substantial a degree by more theoretically inclined computer scientists. Moreover, given the long time horizons of many experimental projects, sustained funding is as important as adequate levels of funding. As an associate professor at a public university commented:

> The NSF "small science" model does not work for my kind of research. I need to replace equipment more often, my work cries for staff programmer support, I need more like 6 to 8 graduate students rather than 1. . . . I would estimate that I need on the order of $300,000 per year funding to carry out the kind of quality experimental systems building and measurement I know I am capable of. Not having the resources implies a distinct waste of talent, especially when you multiply out by all the researchers affected.

Experimentally oriented programs have tended to thrive in recent years, and in today's application-oriented, task-oriented environment it is often easier to obtain funding for ECSE than for theoretical work. For example, among the agencies that fund ECSE (principally NSF, the Office of Naval Research (ONR), and ARPA), there have been some especially successful experimentally oriented programs. The Microelectronics Information Processing Systems (MIPS) Division of NSF's Computer Information Science and Engineering (CISE) Directorate has had an experimental systems program that provides sufficiently large and sustained funding to permit a serious implementation effort. ARPA created and sustains an implementation ser-

---

[11] Such a course is not without its own hazards, such as establishing one's own identity as an independent researcher.

vice for metal-oxide semiconductors (MOSIS), making it possible for academic researchers to design silicon chips near the cutting edge of technology. ARPA also funds projects at a high enough level to build substantial artifacts. ONR has been effective at tracking emerging technological trends and funding exploratory projects.

Although the greater funding needs of experimentalists have been recognized to a considerable degree, a number of problems remain. One of the most vexing for junior faculty members is the difficulty of obtaining external "start-up" funding. A junior faculty member will receive funding in his or her second year only if fortunate enough to get a successful proposal through the system in the very first year as faculty. Such a faculty member would be fortunate indeed, because beginning assistant professors have not, in general, established their professional reputations. For these individuals, only the agencies that accept unsolicited proposals provide realistic funding options, of which the NSF is the most prominent.[12]

Two NSF programs, in particular, have been essential to junior ECSE faculty: the National Young Investigator (NYI; formerly the Presidential Young Investigator (PYI)) program and the Research Initiation Awards (RIA) program.[13] Whereas the former is a foundation-wide program, the RIA is special to the CISE directorate and to engineering. The NYI/PYI program has allowed junior ECSE faculty to support several graduate students and rudimentary equipment for a long enough time that significant work can be accomplished, and the RIA program has provided summer salary or support for one or two graduate students.

At the same time, both programs are highly competitive, meaning that only a few faculty will succeed in winning an award in their first year after graduation, and less than half will ever receive such an award in their eligibility period.[14] In addition, although there is no explicit prohibition against new graduates being funded by other agencies, the reality is that one needs a research track record to be successful in most cases.[15]

Research supported by other mission-oriented agencies such as ARPA is more concentrated in a smaller number of institutions with well-

---

[12] Submitting proposals in collaboration with a senior faculty member may increase the likelihood that an unsolicited proposal to an agency other than NSF will be funded, although the potential risks of being caught in the shadows of a more senior researcher are quite real.

[13] There are a few other possibilities for new Ph.D.s to receive funding from NSF (e.g., the Presidential Faculty Fellow program, special programs directed at minorities, and the regular grant programs), but these are not realistic options for most new faculty.

established reputations. It is a common perception at universities with less established reputations that such agencies fund mainly large projects with senior people as principal investigators at a few large schools, making it particularly difficult for the single ECSE faculty member at a small school to obtain funding. One faculty member (an associate professor at a large public university) noted that seeking support from mission-oriented agencies entails an additional set of barriers:

> I am seeking support from DARPA [Defense Advanced Research Projects Agency] and other similar agencies, but that comes with a whole additional set of problems (somewhat closed communities that are hard to break into, having to be more responsive to very specific agency desires, and generally more personal "overhead" in dealing with them).

---

[14] This situation can be put into perspective by the following snapshot of PYI and RIA funding within the NSF CISE Directorate. The three primary research divisions of CISE responsible for monitoring PYI and RIA funding are the divisions for Microelectronics Information Processing Systems (MIPS); Information, Robotics, and Intelligent Systems (IRIS); and Computer and Computation Research (CCR). The number of grants of each type being monitored by each division for 1990-1991 were as follows:

| CISE Division | Type of Award | Theoretical | Experimental | Total |
|---|---|---|---|---|
| MIPS (1991) | RIA | 4 | 25 | 29 |
|  | PYI | 5 | 33 | 38 |
| CCR (1990) | RIA | 11 | 22 | 33 |
|  | PYI | 23 | 30 | 53 |
| IRIS (1991) | RIA | 3 | 34 | 37 |
|  | PYI | 32 | 2 | 34 |
|  | All RIAs | 18 | 81 | 99 |
|  | All PYIs | 30 | 95 | 125 |
|  | Totals | 48 | 176 | 224 |

---

SOURCE: National Science Foundation and Taulbee Report for 1990-1991 (see Gries, David, and Dorothy Marsh. 1992. "The 1990-1991 Taulbee Survey," *Computing Research News* 4 (January):8).

Because these figures reflect multiyear grants, an estimate of a single year's awards can be made. For example, PYI awards have a five-year duration, and so there are approximately 25 awards in a given year in all areas of computing. Similarly, the RIAs were two-year awards in this period, giving a number of approximately 50 per year. Thus, in a given year, approximately 75 research awards are made to new faculty. In the 1990-1991 academic year, 247 new Ph.D.s in computer science or computer engineering took faculty positions in those fields at Ph.D.-granting institutions.

[15] A rare exception is the ONR Young Investigator program.

Industrial support often suffers from a similar trend. Although industry has often collaborated in research with an academic partner (e.g., Intel's successful collaborations with Carnegie Mellon, Caltech, and the Massachusetts Institute of Technology), industry leaders also tend to concentrate their research expenditures at a very few top schools. Personal contacts are important. Unless they are carefully chosen, projects of direct interest to industry may have too little scholarly content to contribute positively to a faculty member's career.

Finally, as the economy has tightened, industry donations of equipment appear to have declined, and there is little evidence that a turnaround will be forthcoming. Software donations are even more problematic. Although software plays a critical role in almost all types of experimental projects, software donations to universities are relatively rare, even compared with hardware donations.[16]

Even when industry donations of equipment can be obtained, they do not by themselves solve the infrastructure problem. In fact, some "free gifts" end up being very costly in terms of expended time and labor. As described elsewhere in this report, a single research project attempts to innovate in only one particular aspect of a system. To develop, test, and evaluate the mechanism or concept, the system will rely on existing software and hardware as much as possible. If the software support is inadequate (e.g., for compilers, operating system, device drivers, communication), the researcher must expend considerable time and effort filling in the missing pieces. Moreover, "free" equipment rarely comes with free maintenance. Most equipment is either costly, very time-consuming, or both, to maintain.[17] A new faculty member with minimal financial support may not have the funds to maintain donated equipment.

The conclusion from this rather grim funding description is that new ECSE faculty members are not likely to have research support based on their own research ideas during the early years of their careers. This presents them with a major challenge to find the equipment, graduate student funding, and infrastructure support needed to conduct a credible experimental research program.

---

[16] Informal inquiries by the committee among potential donors of software suggest that the underlying reason for the paucity of software donations is related, at least in part, to the lack of tax incentives for such donations. Charitable contributions of merchandise entitle the donor to deduct from income only the manufacturing or production cost of such artifacts (without any mention of associated R&D costs). Of course, the manufacturing cost of a software artifact (the cost of copying some tapes or disks and some manuals) is nearly zero when R&D costs are ignored. Thus, software donations seem not to have a significant benefit to the donor.

[17] For example, in NSF infrastructure grants, cumulative maintenance costs are often 50 percent or more of the equipment costs.

## Time

Almost all schools adhere to a six-year probationary period, after which a tenure decision on junior faculty members must be made. Given the character of ECSE work, this constraint places particular burdens on academic experimental computer scientists and engineers, as compared to their theoretical colleagues. The delays inherent in ECSE work, described below, make it rare for junior ECSE faculty to produce enough in that time to become widely known throughout the CS&E community. Except in the rarest of cases, the tenure candidate will be recognized only among his or her direct community of researchers.

One solution to this problem would be to extend the probationary period for ECSE faculty members. However, a serious exploration of that solution would have required the committee to address larger political issues beyond the scope of its charge or resources. Instead, the committee chose to identify the issues that make ECSE particularly time-consuming, in the hope that tenure and promotion committees would take these issues into account when considering junior ECSE faculty members for tenure.

### Building Complex Artifacts

Artifacts are complex, and it may take years to design and implement an artifact with which one can experiment. The sheer effort of producing a 100,000-line program or a 200,000-transistor chip design may consume a substantial amount of an assistant professor's probationary time.

### Building a Research Laboratory

A new faculty member with research interests in ECSE that are different from those already represented in his or her department must build a research team from scratch (i.e., training the graduate students). In general, it takes several semesters to attract talented students and train them in experimentally oriented systems courses. Graduate students must usually complete several smaller projects before they have the background, skills, and knowledge to tackle dissertation-scale work.

Laboratory development is also time-consuming for the beginning assistant professor, except in those rare cases in which a department has an existing faculty member with very similar laboratory requirements and the willingness and capacity to share existing laboratory facilities with a new faculty member. If no seed funding for the beginning assistant professor is provided by the institution, the process may well take much more than one year because it takes at least one year to acquire funding.

At a minimum, developing a new laboratory involves raising the necessary seed funding, contacting and negotiating with vendors, negotiating maintenance agreements with the vendor or university support, negotiating and paying for software licenses, funding upgrades on software and hardware, and training graduate students to carry out daily management of the system (e.g., performing regular backups) and to use it effectively. Even after the laboratory is established, it remains an ongoing management activity for the faculty to deal with issues such as laboratory organization, facility enhancement, dealing with broken facilities and upgrades, and student management.

### Building Industrial Relationships

In ECSE, much of the most advanced work is being done in industry, and the cooperation between industry and academia is essential to the well-being of the field. This fact introduces several problems for the young faculty member. It takes a long time to develop industrial contacts because, in general, industry prefers to work with a few well-known people at well-established schools, and in some cases, industrial laboratory managers are quite intolerant of academic research. Consider the following comment from an assistant professor at a public university:

> After I am tenured I will be willing to work on longer-term projects. Currently I only begin a research project if I am confident that I can have it sufficiently completed that I can publish a conference paper within a year. Many of my ideas cannot be completed in that timeframe. After tenure I'll also be willing to put more time into developing a relationship with industry. It takes time that I cannot afford now to develop those relationships, though I think they would be very valuable both for my research and for industry.

### Graduating Doctoral Students

The best available data indicate that the average time to complete a Ph.D. in computer science is 6.4 years.[18] Even if this figure characterized the time to Ph.D. for graduate students in experimental com-

---

[18] Computer Science and Telecommunications Board. 1992. *Computing the Future.* National Academy Press, Washington, D.C., p. 244.

puter science (it most likely understates the time), in the six-year probationary period, a junior ECSE faculty member might have only one completed Ph.D. student. In fact, often very good experimentalists have no completed Ph.D. students at the time of the tenure decision, although it is not unreasonable to expect them to have several Ph.D. students nearing graduation. When universities consider only the number of completed Ph.D.s as an important criterion for tenure (and do not take into account students in the pipeline), ECSE faculty are placed at a serious disadvantage.

### Recovering from Wrong Turns and Dead Ends, and from Being Scooped

It is a natural consequence of any research that occasionally a dead-end path is pursued or an unfortunate trade-off is made. A mistake may well be the result of one of several "nontechnical" factors unrelated to the basic idea being studied: a hardware vendor does not deliver or does not perform as expected; funding runs out; key project participants leave; the technology was inadequate to the task. An equally frustrating event is that the work being performed by one researcher is "scooped" by another (i.e., it is published or otherwise publicly released before the first researcher has had time to announce the result).

In the normal course of events, the researcher, having made an error or having been scooped, must back up and proceed forward with the corrected decision, or simply turn his or her attention to a new problem. However, for the ECSE researcher, the consequences of bad decisions or being scooped are particularly severe, because of the large amount of time that the researcher may have invested without productive and creditable results.

### Building a Reputation

As noted in Chapter 1, a great deal of ECSE research is conveyed to the community through the diffusion of artifacts. In terms of time, the diffusion process for artifacts is much more costly than the usual journal publication route, in which the entire relevant community learns of a significant article when it first appears in print. As a result, reputations in ECSE tend to take longer to establish.

In addition, it is traditional in the biological and physical sciences for both experimentalists and theoreticians to take postdoctoral positions for several years after receipt of the Ph.D. Individuals in these fields use this time to concentrate on their research and thereby get a "head start" on establishing their reputation in the relevant research community before the tenure decision is made. ECSE has mostly had no such tradition (although theoreticians in computer science as well as specialists in artificial intelligence are beginning to develop one), and new Ph.D.s in ECSE often take assistant professorships upon graduation. They therefore do not receive the benefits of a comparable time period in which to establish their reputations. The situation may be changing, however, as regular faculty jobs in ECSE become more scarce.

## THE RELATIONSHIP OF RESEARCH SCALE TO INFRASTRUCTURE NEEDS

Infrastructure needs are determined largely by the scale of the research to be supported. Research in ECSE can be conducted at different scales of funding and effort. A small-scale project could be funded at the level of perhaps $100,000 for two years and require one or two person-years to complete; the research "team" might consist of a single investigator at almost any university and a part-time project secretary or assistant. A large-scale project might cost several million dollars per year for several years and require dozens of person-years to complete. It is inherently collaborative, and the research team might consist of several principal investigators, a dozen graduate students, a few technical staff members, and a full-time administrative officer. Such large-scale projects can usually be housed at only a few select universities with the necessary institutional resources and capabilities. Box 2.2 contains examples of small-, medium-, and large-scale ECSE research projects.

Obviously, large-scale ECSE research makes greater demands on infrastructure than small-scale research; it also inevitably requires the presence of collaborative teams. Thus, it is clear that not all types of ECSE can flourish equally well in all academic environments. Scaling project size to resources and facilities available at any particular institution is an important consideration for every researcher. Indeed, the ability to choose significant problems appropriately when faced with such constraints may be a distinguishing mark of creativity and thoughtfulness in a faculty member.

Similar considerations also apply to the question of time. It is undeniable that large-scale systems projects take a long time to complete. However, ECSE researchers also have the option of choosing smaller-scale experimental problems that do not take as long to complete. Undertaking large-scale ECSE research that is carefully structured so that meaningful intermediate outputs can be obtained is also an option in many cases.

---

### BOX 2.2 Scales of ECSE Research

*Small-scale ECSE research.* The program synthesizer, undertaken in the early 1970s, was the forerunner of the programming environments that are in use in most modern software engineering projects today, and yet it was performed at a scale of perhaps six to seven person-years (one faculty member and one graduate student) with total funding of about $150,000 over its lifetime.

*Medium-scale ECSE research.* The Sprite operating system, described in Chapter 1, was undertaken in the 1970s. It lasted four to five years, involved two full-time-equivalent faculty and several graduate students, and consumed perhaps $1 million over its entire lifetime.

*Large-scale ECSE research.* The Multics project was a large-scale systems research project undertaken in the 1960s to develop a scalable time-shared computer utility. Over its eight-year R&D lifetime, its ARPA-supported budget was on the order of $2 million per year; in addition, the Bell Telephone Laboratories and General Electric (later Honeywell) contributed comparable resources during this period. At MIT the development effort in addition to staff involved about a dozen faculty members and perhaps two dozen graduate students. Although commercialization of Multics was only moderately successful—a peak of 77 sites worldwide—concepts researched and developed through the Multics project (such as virtual memory, mapped files, dynamic linking, protection mechanisms) play key roles in many operating systems today. The UNIX operating system in particular built heavily on the Multics experience.

---

## SUMMARY

Without adequate infrastructure, many ECSE faculty are not able to fulfill their true potential. There are many facets to this infrastructure. The availability of general computing environments in the form of workstations has improved immensely over the past 10 years. However, as described in this chapter, a workstation alone is not sufficient to carry out interesting and important experimental research in software systems, let alone hardware.

The bottom line is that on the basis of infrastructure considerations alone, most ECSE faculty who are trying to pursue important work cannot hope to achieve the same publication or completed-Ph.D. records as their theoretical colleagues: they encounter unavoidable delays before start-up, the work is more time-consuming along the way, and their unavoidable dependence on factors such as graduate students and external vendors can add significant delays or drag to the process.

# 3
# Educational Dimensions of
# Academic ECSE

Although it is the research dimension of the academic experience on which the distinguishing characteristics of the experimental computer science and engineering (ECSE) discipline have their greatest effect, the educational dimension of academic ECSE also imposes special demands on faculty.

## KEEPING COURSES CURRENT

Courses in ECSE cover material that changes much more rapidly than the material in theoretical courses, owing to the continuing rapid advances in technologies. For example, the design of VLSI circuits was in its infancy 10 years ago; today courses in VLSI design are a basic staple of many computer science departments. Courses on the design of high-performance computer architectures are another example. Rapid technological change means that ECSE faculty typically spend more time each year upgrading courses to incorporate new material; course notes, laboratory facilities, and software do not have long lifetimes. For the same reason, ECSE faculty often cannot rely on textbooks alone (and sometimes not at all) to adequately cover material because of its rapidly changing nature.

An additional complication is the laboratory component of ECSE courses. ECSE shares with many science and engineering courses the need to develop, maintain, and upgrade laboratory facilities, but laboratory equipment for ECSE courses can be expensive, relative to its short useful life, especially for courses in which the effective presentation of material depends on equipment that is near the state of the art. An example would be a computer graphics course, in which certain techniques for realistically rendering three-dimensional images require very large amounts of computing power if those images are to display in real time.

In addition, if undergraduate students in computer science are to be employable by industry upon graduation, they must have some reasonable familiarity with the equipment that they will encounter in industry. This is not to say that the equipment of ECSE laboratories must be upgraded in lockstep with that of industry; however, over time the department whose teaching laboratory equipment does not keep pace with technological changes occurring in industry will find its graduates poorly prepared. Thus, a continuing effort to upgrade (rather than just maintain) laboratory facilities is a demand faced by ECSE faculty, but not by faculty in disciplines with a stable core of "classic" experiments.

Some schools recognize the need to treat the educational dimension of CS&E as a laboratory science, and they provide meaningful staff support in the form of laboratory technicians, programmers, and the like. However, other institutions lack such staff support, and in their ECSE laboratories development, maintenance, and upgrading tasks fall to the faculty themselves.

## EVALUATING STUDENT WORK

Not surprisingly, student work in ECSE courses has qualities that mirror the discipline itself, including complexity, reliance on artifacts, and technological sensitivity. Moreover, these courses often represent a substantial portion of the design component of the curriculum, especially the advanced specialty courses.

Students produce software and hardware artifacts in almost all ECSE courses as part of their homework. For example, students may write drivers for input/output devices in a course on operating systems, or design a chip in a VLSI design course. In general, there are many more ways to carry out a laboratory assignment than are present in the abstract systems that are the focus of typical problem sets. This multiplicity is due to the greater number of variables and the need to attend to all of the details in a real physical system.

The result is that no simple key can be used to decide the correctness of the homework. Programs or circuit designs are not simply correct or wrong; correctness is only one of many properties that must be evaluated to assign a grade to this work. Properties such as efficiency, maintainability, modularity, and readability cannot be evaluated by looking at the output of the program. For example, a very convoluted and unnecessarily intricate program may produce valid answers to a set of test data, although a human grader would reasonably downgrade such a program for its unnecessary complexity. As a result, the entire program (data structures, algorithms, procedure calls, even syntax) has to be studied in detail and reasoned through line by line. Absent cheating, no two programs will be the same.

Although laboratory exercises for low-level classes can sometimes be packaged well enough to facilitate grading, project classes and advanced graduate classes cannot be similarly packaged. A typical project submission by a four-person team might involve a program consisting of 10,000 lines of source code and hundreds of pages of documentation and analysis, and a faculty member might have to grade 15 or 20 such projects in one course, or even more. Finally, reading and understanding such projects are considerably more difficult than, say, reading and understanding term papers.

The end result is that preparing and evaluating laboratory experiments and other design projects are extremely time-consuming, more so than for most lecture/recitation courses. Thus, ECSE faculty typically need more teaching assistant support than do faculty teaching courses that do not require projects or design work.

## STUDENT-FACULTY RATIOS

Teaching burdens tend to be higher in computer science departments than in other departments. Although the number of course preparations per semester required of ECSE faculty is likely to be the same as that of other faculty in CS&E or in other science or engineering disciplines, the number of students per class tends to be much larger. For example, the number of degrees awarded per year in computer-related fields (including computer science, computer engineering, and information sciences) per full-time faculty member is more than double that of science and engineering departments taken as a whole.[1] Moreover, in recent years service teaching loads (i.e., nonmajors taking computer science courses) have increased substantially.

---

[1] Computer Science and Telecommunications Board. 1992. *Computing the Future.* National Academy Press, Washington, D.C., p. 258.

## SUPERVISING NON-PH.D. GRADUATE STUDENTS

ECSE faculty tend to be responsible for more graduate students than their theoretical colleagues. Although at least some of the time spent supervising Ph.D. students contributes directly to the faculty member's research, as is the case for non-ECSE faculty, the situation is quite different with respect to master's students, whom ECSE faculty tend to take on in relatively large numbers. (These students are frequently continuing education students from industry.) Master's student projects may or may not contribute to the research of an ECSE faculty member, but they nonetheless require supervision and guidance, often at an intensity comparable to that required by Ph.D. students, although not for as long.

# 4

# Evaluating Research in ECSE

Why does experimental computer science and engineering (ECSE) flourish on some campuses and struggle on others? Some of the differences are the result of historical accident, but the issue is much deeper than that. Many experimentalists believe that the academic career deck is stacked against them. The committee also found that publication practices in ECSE emphasize conference publication over archival journal publication, a fact likely to be negatively interpreted by the "paper counters" of university promotion and tenure committees.

Furthermore, there are differing interpretations within the computer science and engineering (CS&E) field itself of what constitutes scholarly work. The issue can perhaps be constructively introduced by reporting the results of a small, informal survey in which about 20 computer scientists from around the country were asked by the chair of the committee whether they thought a faculty member should "get tenure for inventing the mouse."

The mouse is an example of an artifact that has realized the goals of ECSE and exemplifies an ECSE research success. It is an encapsulation of ECSE research knowledge in the following ways:

- The mouse falls within the scope of ECSE, having mechanical, electronic, and software components concerned with human-computer interfaces.
- The concepts underlying the mouse fundamentally improve the functionality of the human-computer interface.

- The concepts were shown to be "better" quantitatively.
- The mouse has had a significant impact as witnessed by a variety of subsequent implementations, improvements, and applications, as well as widespread use.

Despite these qualities, the replies to the chair's informal survey correlated strongly with whether the respondent was an experimentalist (yes) or a theoretician (no). The question exposed fundamental differences of opinion concerning the nature of research accomplishments. It also emphasizes that the research of junior faculty members—either theoreticians or experimentalists—whose senior faculty are predominantly in the other area might not be fully appreciated at promotion time.

In this chapter two general questions of evaluation are considered. The first concerns how CS&E implements its quality standards for research. Treating this matter entails a careful review of publication forums and traditions in ECSE. The second concerns differences in experimental and theoretical research and how these differences affect a professor's evaluation.

## PUBLICATION AND OTHER FORMS OF DISSEMINATION

The scholarly articulation of a contribution is a key characteristic of research, and all intellectual communities have mechanisms through which new knowledge and information are disseminated and explicated. In addition, certain communities place considerable value on establishing priority and claiming credit for new ideas and innovations. Not surprisingly, the particular mechanisms used by any given community depend on the efficacy with which those mechanisms facilitate the dissemination of information and the establishment of priority.

Communication with other researchers in ECSE has several aspects. As in all fields, the first goal is to convey the content of the work. Next in importance, the academic researcher in ECSE wishes to convince other researchers or developers to *use* an idea or implementation. This requires the researcher to demonstrate the worth of the idea. Such arguments can be made on a quantitative or qualitative basis, although the former is likely to be more easily conveyed. The idea must be reported in great enough detail to allow others to reproduce it, or the actual implementation that embodies the idea (i.e., the artifact) must be provided to the community. Reproduction of experimental data may also require the availability of a genuine implementation.

For potential adopters of an idea, both timeliness and quality of publication are important. Timeliness is critical because ECSE moves so rapidly, and ideas that take a long time to reach potential users often become irrelevant or obsolete. Quality is important because new ideas must be well explained, as well as convincing in their technical arguments, with comparative discussion of other approaches and often extensive quantitative evidence that substantiates the merit of an approach. A strong refereeing process plays a valuable role in identifying important and innovative ideas and in promoting those that are well justified. It also helps to ensure that earlier work is properly attributed and that a claimed innovation is in fact new work.

Researchers in ECSE use several forums for the publication of their research: conference proceedings, archival journals, technical reports. As importantly, they also disseminate information through a variety of "nonstandard" channels (e.g., distributing software artifacts, creating and distributing videotapes, presenting demonstrations off-site) so that they can demonstrate intangible and dynamic properties of artifacts for other researchers who wish to interact directly with their work. Such nonstandard channels are critical to ECSE research, especially for proof-of-concept or proof-of-existence artifacts.

## Publications

Conference proceedings and journal articles are the most important publication channels and are discussed in greater detail below. Technical reports provide a detailed description of work in progress that enables other researchers to collaborate with the author(s) and validate and enhance the work. They are the main vehicle for immediate distribution of technical information and gaining feedback on the value of a work. Under most circumstances, technical reports are not refereed beyond the immediate department; in some cases, such publication requires at most the approval of the department head. Technical reports are freely distributed, and many technical reports are available on-line (via Internet access).

A substantial majority of respondents to the CRA-CSTB survey of ECSE faculty preferred conferences as the means of dissemination by which to achieve maximum intellectual impact; many fewer preferred journals. Conferences were preferred primarily because of timeliness and, to a lesser extent, the better audience offered by conferences (i.e., they are better focused). Researchers who favored journals were almost equally split among three motivations: university recognition, stronger refereeing, and a wider audience.

Although researchers favored conference publication by a significant majority, a large majority of the researchers surveyed also indicated their belief that journals were much more effective in gaining university recognition. Most indicated that the reason for this was that university administrators put more emphasis on journals; very few indicated that journals had higher prestige or greater impact.[1] Put differently, only a small number of respondents to the CRA-CSTB survey agreed that the best publication vehicle to gain university recognition was also the best vehicle for intellectual impact on the field; the remainder felt that there was a conflict between these two vehicles.

## Journals

The leading journals in ECSE include the Association of Computing Machinery (ACM) journals, the Institute of Electrical and Electronics Engineers (IEEE) transactions as well as the more selective IEEE magazines, and the leading independent private journals such as the *Journal of Parallel and Distributed Computing* or *Artificial Intelligence*.[2] These journals are characterized by a rigorous and demanding refereeing procedure and rather selective publication (although it varies considerably by publication).

The primary characteristic of these journal publications is a thorough and often lengthy review process. (See Appendix B for a fuller discussion.) This review process enables the referees to request changes to a paper and to ensure that such changes are carried out with the help of the editor. Typically, papers are reviewed by three outside referees, although in many cases one of the referees may fail to produce a report, leaving the editor with only two recommendations.

---

[1] In a "President's Letter" in 1988, Paul Abrahams (then president of the Association of Computing Machinery) pointed out that "archival journals have also come to serve another, less healthy purpose: providing credentials for those who would publish in them. The pressure to publish is intense in academia. . . . A strong publication list is usually a prerequisite to tenure in a first-rate university. Within the research community more generally, publication in archival journals brings reward and recognition. It is not enough to be published; it is necessary to be published in the right places." Abrahams, Paul. 1988. "Our Archival Journals," *Communications of the ACM* 31(4):370-371.

[2] *Artificial Intelligence* is perhaps the leading journal dealing with this subject, but it is not devoted exclusively or even primarily to experimental work. Artificial intelligence (AI) is a subdiscipline of computer science and engineering with both experimental and theoretical components. For purposes of this report, the experimental component of AI is included in ECSE.

On the basis of referee reports, the editor makes a decision to accept the paper, to request minor or major revisions, or to reject the paper. When major revisions are required, most editors send the paper back to at least a subset of the original referees. When minor revisions are required, the editor either examines the paper or sends it back to the referees.

The questions on which journal reviewers tend to focus are, Are the results right? Are the weaknesses fixable? and, What value will this have for posterity? Journal reviewers typically spend considerable time understanding the argument presented in the paper and finding ways to strengthen it. Even highly favorable reviews of a paper usually have extensive comments about how to improve it.

Many people believe that most papers are significantly improved by the refereeing and revision process. Among the improvements are clearer exposition, higher level of completeness and correctness, and better comparisons with other work. Editors of major journals have observed that papers written by less experienced authors are often seriously lacking in one of these areas.

Journal papers typically are not constrained by length, although budget limitations have led to requests for authors to shorten papers or to divide them into two parts for publication. Journals are typically classified as private journals or professional society journals. Of these, the society journals are regarded as more prestigious. However, many authors in ECSE are drawn to private journals because they tend to publish more rapidly, while still maintaining high standards for refereeing.

In ECSE, journal articles have special value in consolidating and summarizing work for the long term. Because there are few limitations on length and because of the greater emphasis on completeness, possibly at the expense of timeliness, journal articles are an ideal mechanism to review what has been learned throughout a major portion of a project's lifetime, and to place that knowledge into a broader context.[3] By contrast, journal articles are less suitable as a means for disseminating information about intermediate results whose long-term significance may become clear only when the full context of the work can be presented.

---

[3] The following is a good example of an archival journal article serving this role: Davidson, Jack W., and Christopher W. Fraser. 1984. "Code Selection Through Object Code Optimization," *ACM Transactions on Programming Languages and Systems* 6(4):505-526. This paper is the "consolidation" paper for the peephole optimizer described in Chapter 1.

## Conferences

The leading conferences in ECSE are typically carefully refereed (although by a different process than is used for journals) and have high standards for acceptance, as indicated by relatively low rates of acceptance. Conferences that meet these standards include the International Symposium on Computer Architecture (ISCA), the conference on Architectural Support for Programming Languages and Operating Systems (ASPLOS), the conference on Programming Language Design and Implementation (PLDI), the Symposium on Operating System Principles (SOSP), and the SIGCOMM and SIGGRAPH conferences. Papers published as part of these conferences are of comparable significance to those published in the best of journals.

The paper selection process for these conferences relies heavily on the program committee as the primary referees. Although external referees are also used, typically at least one-half of the refereeing process is handled by the program committee. A paper usually receives at least four, and often five, reviews. (For example, a recent ISCA conference averaged 4.4 reviews for each of 209 submitted papers.) Because these are the leading conferences, the program committee generally consists of highly respected individuals. Thus, this round of refereeing is often as thorough and discriminating (sometimes more so) as the refereeing done by journal publications. Indeed, because conferences are often unable to request extensive revision of submitted papers, strong papers with flaws are often rejected, whereas for a journal they would be revised for additional consideration. Because the conference selection process is relatively rapid, a paper that is rejected can be revised and resubmitted to another conference or to a journal. The ability to do this depends on having high-quality feedback on the papers.

The major disadvantage of the conference review and selection process is the lack of an opportunity to review revisions to papers. This capability is the major additional quality control that can be exercised by journals. The committee's data show that a second review is required for about one-half of the papers published in journals such as ACM's *Transactions on Computer Systems* and *Transactions on Programming Languages and Systems*. To provide the opportunity for improving papers in a similar fashion to that achieved by a second refereeing, several conferences have adopted a method called shepherding, in which papers that are worthy of acceptance but have some problems are handled by an appointed member of the program committee. This person, called the shepherd, works with the authors to convey additional comments from the program committee and referees and reviews the revised paper prior to publication. The idea of shepherding arose in connection with the SOSP conference, where it is used heavily (often more than one-half of the papers are shepherded), but it has recently been adopted by other conferences, although usually on a smaller scale (with only about one-quarter of the papers being shepherded).

The major disadvantage of conference publication is the limitation in length. Many conferences limit the final paper as well as the version submitted for refereeing. For example, the submitted summaries are often limited to 5,000 to 7,500 words. With such limits, the submitted version may differ somewhat from the final printed paper. Experience has shown that well-written papers can fit within the limit and still contain enough information to allow referees to make an accurate judgment, if the program committee understands the area well. Papers that require substantial additional background may not easily fit within these constraints, or within the final length limitations imposed when the paper is accepted.

A minor disadvantage of conference publication is the somewhat limited distribution, compared with that of journals. Conference attendees, who generally include the majority of researchers actively studying a topic, all receive a copy. Additionally, ACM's special interest groups (SIGs) often send a copy to all members. For example, ACM's Special Interest Group on Computer Architecture (SIGARCH) sends a copy of the ISCA and ASPLOS proceedings to all of its members. However, not all SIGs follow this custom, and even for those that do, broad circulation is not customary for all of the conferences sponsored by the SIG. Finally, libraries have in the past not always appreciated the importance of conference publication to ECSE, and so conference holdings at many libraries are often incomplete or nonexistent.

The major advantage of conference publication is the greatly reduced time to publication. The typical leading conferences have submission dates that are roughly six or seven months before the conference date. The leading journals have average submission-to-publication times of more than two years.[4] This time differential is discussed further in Appendix B.

Like journals, conferences vary widely in their selectivity. In addition to the highly selective smaller conferences, there is also a set

---

[4] The long publication delays for journals arise primarily because of long referee delays. Several journal editors have tried to address the problems and streamline the refereeing process. In addition, journals have been developed that focus on articles of current interest and explicitly try to shorten publication delays (such as the new ACM *Letters on Programming Languages and Systems*).

of conferences that, while demanding, tend to have larger programs and multiple, parallel tracks. Because many of these conferences are large, the refereeing process is necessarily less focused and cannot be as carefully done. These conferences probably compare in selectivity to the less demanding journals. There are also workshops and informally refereed conferences with even lower selectivity. The better papers presented in such workshops are often revised and extended for submission to a leading conference or journal.

Although the overall selectivity of a conference is one indicator of the quality of papers presented, it is at best a gross measure. Thus, a conference for which 30 papers of 100 are accepted (acceptance rate of 30 percent) may well have a higher overall quality than one for which 50 of 200 papers are accepted (acceptance rate of 25 percent). Accordingly, acceptance rate is only one factor to consider in determining the intellectual importance of any given conference.

The questions on which conference paper reviewers tend to focus have a different character from those of journal reviewers. Although concerned with technical accuracy, conference reviewers tend to pay much more attention to questions such as, Is this work important? Will others in the community care about this work? and, Is it timely? As noted earlier, conference referees tend to prefer outright rejection rather than extensive revision because of their tight time constraints, although they often make comments intended to strengthen the paper. These two factors —importance/timeliness and tight reviewing deadlines—mean that papers rejected by important conferences would often have passed the quality threshold for journal publication, although perhaps with revisions required.

Many of the same observations about timeliness and selectivity were made in a study of information needs in the sciences undertaken by the Research Libraries Group. Its study of publication and publication dissemination in computer science states the following: "In computer science, conferences are the venue for presenting important new research, and competition for the opportunity to do so is intense. In fact, presenting a paper at the more prestigious conferences is preferred to publication in a leading journal."[5] This source also indicates the important advantage that conferences offer in time to publication, as does the Abrahams letter cited above.[6]

---

[5] Gould, Constance, and Karla Pearce. Undated. *Information Needs in the Sciences: An Assessment.* Report prepared for the Program for Research Information Management, Research Libraries Group, Inc., Mountain View, Calif., p. 71.

[6] Abrahams. 1988. "Our Archival Journals."

Conference proceedings have one additional advantage over journal publication—they are presented to live audiences, typically in 20 to 30 minutes. Feedback from the audience, both as part of the formal presentation and in informal conversations in the hall or over meals, often has a direct and immediate impact on the progress of a project.

## Artifacts as a Medium for Dissemination

Because an artifact often embodies aspects of the intellectual content of ECSE research that may be intangible, it is important to consider how this content is communicated to the research community.

Artifacts released to the research community are a very different medium from publications. Where publications describe work, artifacts are themselves the work. As noted earlier, good publications pass through peer review that typically involves the judgments of several reviewers and a few editors. Artifacts must instead pass a "marketplace" test, in which the relevant community as a whole votes "with its feet" (or its keyboards!) and defines work with significant impact. People are often most easily persuaded that an artifact provides better functionality by trying it out rather than by reading about it. Note that in terms of "getting the details right," nothing is more exacting than the artifact itself—it has to work!

How can impact be measured? The principle underlying impact in ECSE is simple: an artifact or an idea has impact if it changes the way other people work. Useful artifacts are by definition useful to many people. Other potential measures of impact include how long a given artifact has been used, how many people spend substantial time modifying and enhancing it, and how many other pieces of experimental research build on it, although none of these measures are easy to obtain or even to define precisely.[7]

One immediate consequence of the focus on impact is that the importance and significance of a given research contribution may not

---

[7] For example, the number of people "using" an artifact is hard to define. First, it must be users that are measured, because related quantities (e.g., the number of copies requested) do not indicate actual use. Second, some software (e.g., a device driver) may be extremely useful without having any scientific or engineering importance. Third, software differs in the number of potential users, so that, for example, a research tool employed by each of the half dozen research teams in a research specialty may be more significant than a program with dozens of users from among thousands possible. Last, like other aspects of academic life, the number of users may depend more on the effectiveness of the creator in promoting the artifact than on its actual superiority. The number of users cannot be the sole measure of the impact of an artifact.

be immediately evident. This is partly due just to the complexity of artifacts—complicated phenomena often take time to understand no matter how articulate the researcher is. Additionally, even when an idea is evidently good, its impact depends in part on others adopting it, possibly in the creation of artifacts, which in turn takes time and delays when this impact can be measured. Often, the more novel the artifact or idea, the longer it takes to propagate into the community.

Each form of artifact—software, computers, chips, graphic images, databases—carries with it different requirements for dissemination. Nearly all of the nonpublication forms of artifact dissemination rely on the Internet. It is therefore axiomatic that Internet access is a necessity for conducting experimental research.

Typical forms of dissemination are as follows:

- *Software.* The source text of the program and documentation are generally made available for access by anonymous FTP from the host computer of the researcher who produced it.[8] The program is usually free of charge to other researchers. To a lesser degree, software is distributed on magnetic tape provided by the creator, usually for a nominal handling charge, through central libraries such as the Netlib for free, or through secondary sources such as vendors.

- *Computers.* Access to experimental computers is usually provided by researchers to other researchers via "remote log-in," which allows them to run programs on the machine over the Internet without being physically present. In addition to providing access, the researcher must provide documentation on the machine and its specific software, some amount of local disk storage, and some amount of "hand holding."

- *Chip designs.* Standard structures, such as "pads" or the "multibus design frame," are distributed like software via the Internet, but most chip designs are exchanged as designs only rarely. The systems built using the chips may be displayed in some form (e.g., by remote access if they are computers or via demonstrations if they are not).

- *Graphic images.* Dissemination most often takes the form of software to generate the images, but this may require that the recipient have a sophisticated graphics display device. Films and demonstrations at conferences, such as SIGGRAPH, are also important.

- *Computer-aided design (CAD) tools.* Like graphics, distribution is most often in the form of software, but demonstrations at conferences are extremely significant.

---

[8] Anonymous FTP enables remote users to fetch files from a remote computer. FTP stands for file transfer protocol.

- *Data*. A wide range of data is distributed by anonymous FTP over the Internet. Examples include trace data of programs, graphic data sets such as the Utah Tea Pot, benchmark programs such as the Perfect Club (from the University of Illinois) test suites, chip designs for evaluating CAD tools, and test data sets.

These are generic forms of dissemination and do not include personal exchanges between researchers.

The distribution of artifacts is an activity performed by academic ECSE researchers that is not typical in traditional academic disciplines. The distribution of artifacts often demands a substantial commitment of time and resources, and the added work—although valuable to the ECSE community—tends to be intellectually unrewarding.

For example, research software that embodies a novel and useful research idea may be stable and complete enough for tests to be made, measurements to be taken, and papers to be written, and generally be capable of providing answers to intellectually interesting questions. At the same time, it may still be undocumented, incomplete, and quite fragile, with numerous bugs remaining in the system. Such software is useful to those who created it primarily because its creators understand its quirks and "work arounds," and know how to fix it when it breaks; in short, the creators are not unduly hampered by these problems.

On the other hand, outsiders without such knowledge would find the software unusable. Before research-quality software can be disseminated, documentation must be written, bugs removed, omissions filled in, and so on. Additionally, a "distribution" must be planned so that the recipient can install and use the software without intervention by the creators. For a substantial software system, this packaging activity can easily require a person-year; fielding user questions after it has been distributed takes up additional time.

Demonstrations—generally needed for one-of-a-kind hardware or for software running on platforms not widely available—can be a particularly aggravating form of dissemination. In addition to the artifact having to be primped to make it suitable for display (a condition that may require much more effort than originally needed to extract the "research content"), the artifact or the equipment it runs on must be packaged for travel, moved around the country, and set up and interfaced to the local operating environment. Furthermore, it requires a presenter to actually perform the demonstration.

A less bulky, but often no less aggravating, alternative involves using a computing platform at the demonstration site. In this case, although a research software system may have been created by using the home institution's Brand A, Model 2 computer, "minor" differences in the "same" Brand A, Model 2 computer at the demonstration site (e.g., differences in operating system version) may well prevent the demonstration from running smoothly or even at all.

Although the extra work to prepare an artifact for use or access by other researchers may be substantial, it is willingly done by the community and is part of the tradition of the field. The reason, of course, is that distribution is often a necessity for communicating one's ideas and for obtaining professional recognition. As importantly, demonstration to and actual use by independent observers is often the only way to evaluate the true worth of a contribution.

When another party uses an artifact created by the researcher, the researcher receives recognition, but the etiquette of the ECSE community is such that acknowledgment rather than co-authorship is appropriate. Moreover, if the artifact comes into wide use, even acknowledgments become less frequent, especially when it is not the actual program text that is used but rather its underlying algorithm or idea.

## THEORETICIANS' AND EXPERIMENTALISTS'
## VIEWS ON EXPERIMENTAL RESEARCH

The committee believes that accomplishments in ECSE research should be evaluated in the context of the field's tradition as outlined above. However, one of the most serious problems treated in this report concerns a tension that exists between theoretical and experimental computer scientists. This concern manifests itself in the research evaluation process as the question, Is the mouse worthy of tenure? Behind closed doors and never for attribution, one may hear outrageous remarks from both communities: "Experimentalists don't get tenure because their work is no good." "Theory is irrelevant, as are theoreticians." Such comments are clearly counterproductive and demonstrate a lack of appreciation of the real contributions of the other group. Obviously, neither community can make a claim of being the "true" computer researchers, and mutual understanding and respect are essential.

In the committee's view, the crux of the problem is a critical difference in the way the theoretical and experimental research methodologies approach research questions. The problem derives from the enormous complexity that is fundamental to computational problems, as outlined in the discussion of artifacts in Chapter 1. This complexity is confronted in theoretical and experimental research in different ways, as the following oversimplified formulation exhibits.

When presented with a computational problem, a theoretician tries to simplify it to a clean, core question that can be defined with mathematical rigor and analyzed completely. In the simplification, significant parts of the problem may be removed to expose the core question, and simplifying assumptions may be introduced. The goal is to reduce the complexity to a point where it is analytically tractable. As anyone who has tried it knows, theoretical analysis can be extremely difficult, even for apparently straightforward questions.

When presented with a computational problem, an experimentalist tries to decompose it into subproblems, so that each can be solved separately and reassembled for an overall solution. In the decomposition, careful attention is paid to the partitioning so that clean interfaces with controlled interactions remain. The goal is to contain the complexity, and limit the number and variety of mechanisms needed to solve the problem. As anyone who has tried it knows, experimentation can be extremely difficult to get right, requiring science, engineering, and occasionally, good judgment and taste.

The distinction between these two methodologies naturally fosters a point of view that looks with disdain on the research of the other. When experimentalists consider a problem that has been attacked theoretically and study the related theorems that have been produced, they may see the work as irrelevant. After all, the aspects that were abstracted away embodied critical complicating features of the original problem, and these have not been addressed. The theoretician knows no analysis would have been possible had they been retained, whereas the experimentalist sees that "hard parts" of the problem have been left untouched.

Conversely, when theoreticians examine a problem attacked experimentally and spot subproblems for which they recognize theoretical solutions, they may see the work as uninformed and nonscientific. After all, basic, known results of computing have not been applied in this artifact, and so the experimentalist is not doing research, just "hacking." The experimentalist knows that it is the other aspects of the system that represent the research accomplishment, and the fact that it works by using a "wrong" solution implies that the subproblem could not have been too significant anyway (Box 4.1).

So, as by the blind men encountering an elephant, impressions are formed about the significance, integrity, and worth of computing research by its practitioners. Although it is natural for researchers to believe that their own methodology is better, no claim of superiority can be sustained by either. Fundamental advances in CS&E have been achieved by both experiment and theory. Recognizing that fact promotes tolerance and reduces tensions. Unfortunately, these im-

> **BOX 4.1 An Example of Tension Between Theorists and Experimentalists**
>
> An example will help to illustrate the tension between theoretical and experimental computer science. This example is hypothetical, in that its particulars are fictional, although it is grounded in the personal experience of a committee member.
>
> An ECSE faculty member designed a text editor (i.e., a program to arrange text on a page) that incorporates a variety of features that improve its ease of use for novices and also increase its power for expert users. Some of these features are based on novel algorithms and approaches to managing text strings, but the portion of the system that is responsible for displaying the text on the screen uses an algorithm that would be relatively inefficient for displaying large amounts of text (e.g., 100,000 characters) but is perfectly adequate for the amounts of text that will in fact be displayed on all plausible terminal screens (e.g., less than 10,000 characters).
>
> The theorist may criticize the editor on the grounds that the algorithm is known to be inefficient, and that more efficient algorithms are known and should have been used. The experimentalist may well respond that such criticism is irrelevant, because the algorithm used was good enough for all practical purposes, and the editor should be evaluated primarily on the basis of its power and usability.

pressions will likely be used in the process of evaluating professors for promotion and tenure. Although both theoretical and experimental junior faculty are at risk if the senior faculty are predominately of a "different stripe," the problem may be more serious for experimentalists because of the relatively strong antecedents in the field of mathematics (the traditional practices of theoretical computer science are similar to those of mathematics, which are themselves similar to the traditional practices of most universities); also, the relatively recent emergence of experimentation suggests that senior experimentalists are in the minority.

The tension described above was demonstrated in the comments of a number of ECSE faculty responding to the CRA-CSTB survey. Assistant professors wrote,

> It is clear to me that experimental computer science is not considered to be of broad intellectual interest by the vast majority of the senior faculty in my department. [assistant professor at a well-known private university]

> Ironically, I believe that experimental research is frequently viewed as non-scientific. Many people in my department seem to feel that theorems and proofs are the only valid method of argument. [assistant professor at a large public university]

> There is a premium on journal publications, and preferably those with some theoretical leanings. I have decreased the amount of experimental work to orient my work toward this more demonstrably recognizable research contribution. [assistant professor at a well-known private research university]

Opinions expressing the "opposite" impression might be heard from theoreticians in predominately experimental departments, but the CRA-CSTB survey did not sample theoreticians.

For some faculty, an affirmative tenure decision does not change their perception that experimental work is not highly valued. An associate professor at a large public university stated: "I just received tenure this year. I felt under intense pressure to move away from experimental work, and to concentrate on formalization and theory."

Even when the department seems to understand the burdens of the ECSE discipline, it is not always evident to assistant professors that the understanding will be converted to action at promotion time. One insightful assistant professor at a private university observed:

> The department senior faculty and university-level tenure committee do seem to understand that experimental systems work is time-consuming, important and needs to be evaluated differently. On the other hand, there is still a strict demand for demonstration of intellectual ability which is more easily and readily met by focusing on more theoretical journal publications.

Others confirm this:

> Not only does [experimental research] take time and money, but there is no indication that it is appreciated—especially when the primary tenure measure is publication. [assistant professor at a private university]

> I have attempted to do more theoretical work because of the tenuring process even when I feel that the research is not substantially improved by the theoretical aspects and it would have been more productive to spend the same effort on experimental evaluation. [assistant professor at a large public university]

Although it is not possible to determine whether these perceptions are true in fact, the committee believes that they are widely held and that they affect a faculty member's willingness to pursue experimental research as an assistant professor. At the same time, although it is a common belief that experimentalists are disadvantaged at tenure or promotion time in comparison with "equally" qualified theoreticians for the kinds of reasons discussed in this report, the committee made no attempt to document such cases. A tenure decision is based on many considerations, of which research and scholarship is but one (and, as in other areas, it may be that the quality of a researcher's work is low by the standards of the field itself). Other academic duties (e.g., teaching and service) figure into the decision, as do the strength of letters of evaluation, the personalities of the people involved, the prospects for continued scholarly output, student interactions, and so on. Most of these data are not publicly available. It would be impossible, without being present at all of the deliberations and being party to the participants' thoughts, to second-guess an individual tenure decision and assert that someone was denied tenure simply because of prejudice against experimentalists.

## THE EFFECT OF EVALUATION ON PROBLEM CHOICES AND RESEARCH AREA

The practicalities of evaluating ECSE research have substantial impact on how faculty members moving up the career ladder see their own careers. The committee was struck by the considerable intensity of feeling among CRA-CSTB survey respondents that the traditional tenure and promotion (T&P) review process works against their interests and those of the field. The following quotes (all from associate professors at large public universities) illustrate this sentiment:

> It is absolutely apparent to me that tracking the market upon which I depend—that is, staying aware of tools, trends, systems and applications available for use in my research—is quite at odds with the promotion process. Staying on top, as I'd been accustomed, exacts a high cost in time and energy; three years into my position as assistant professor I needed to make a conscious decision to abandon these efforts in favor of work that is technically less crisp, having shorter-term pay off, and perhaps done with less outside impact and applicability . . . . Now having tenure, I have the opportunity to try to return to the front lines of technology.

> [The positive tenure] decision has changed the character of my research to a degree, mostly by giving me the freedom to make the right choice during system development rather than simply the expedient one.

> [The tenure decision] pressed me to publish "something," "anything" decent, even though my systems were not mature, and tended to press me to apply for grants and submit papers regarding work that really was not in the best shape for that.

Such responses indicate an understanding on the part of junior faculty of a career strategy in which one should modulate one's ambitions before the tenure decision is made. Yet it is also clear that many ECSE faculty—junior and senior—consider doing so equivalent to choosing to pursue less important work. That is, because research problems should be selected on the basis of importance, a researcher who chooses not to pursue his or her highest-priority problem is *by definition* working on a less important problem. This is true regardless of the reasons for not pursuing the original problem, (e.g., it is too ambitious to pursue while under tenure pressure).

What is the origin of the sentiments reflected above? In some ways, it is understandable that junior faculty are often frustrated by the need to subordinate their desire to pursue the most promising intellectual paths in order to respond to the immediate demands of producing documentary proof of achievement for the time-limited tenure processes. (The promotion from associate to full professor seems to be less of an issue in this regard.) Individuals who have chosen to pursue careers in a given field have generally done so because they believe they have good ideas to contribute that will move the field forward.

Any field—ECSE included—must allow individuals to undertake high-risk activities for potentially high gain. Indeed, many senior faculty believe that the field progresses most rapidly and vigorously as the result of such activities on a wide range of fronts. In the words of Frederick Brooks of the University of North Carolina, ECSE would clearly benefit from "people with a vision who go aggressively after the vision, heeding no distraction."[9] However, it is also clear that high-risk/high-gain activities should not be the *only* constituent of a field's overall research portfolio. Incremental research with low to moderate risk of failure also has a key role to play in the advancement of any field, although such work is generally far less glamorous. Both types of research are essential to moving ECSE forward.

Almost every researcher would like to be working on high-gain activities if success could be ensured, but the real question for the field is the following: Given that most high-gain research activities have an inherently high risk of failure (as well as being generally more demanding of resources) and that the field will benefit from incremental lower-risk research as well, who should be doing the high-risk/high-gain work?

In one sense, the answer is clear and is recognized by junior and senior faculty alike: tenured faculty have a much greater freedom of action to pursue high-risk research activities, although such freedom is not unlimited. The traditional tenure process in most institutions

---

[9] Personal communication with the committee, October 1992.

provides strong incentives for junior faculty to undertake lower-risk (and correspondingly lower-gain) activities prior to the tenure decision. Given this simple statement of reality, the real problem is how to nurture talent and competence at performing in both lower-risk and higher-risk activities.

The most straightforward strategy for coping with this conflict is for a faculty member to perform lower-risk/lower-payoff work before tenure and higher-risk/higher-payoff work after tenure. This is indeed the approach that many junior ECSE faculty say they have adopted. However, in the absence of any detailed study, it seems that the "high-payoff" accomplishments of ECSE have tended to be those of individuals who "hit for home runs" regardless of their tenure status, thus calling into question this apparently straightforward strategy. In practice, it would seem, many do low-risk research before the tenure decision and continue to do low-risk research even after they have received tenure. As one particularly insightful junior faculty member (an assistant professor at a large public university) said:

> Once I have tenure, my current interest in generating a larger *number* of publications will probably shift toward a smaller number of high-quality publications. Or then, again, it may not. My saddest reflection on the tenure process is that six years is long enough that the shaping that occurs may be permanent.

One aspect of the low-risk strategy worth noting is the difference between a researcher working on projects that are structured in a way that allows for meaningful intermediate output (a desirable mode of research consistent with the discussion above) and a researcher maximizing his or her publication count by adopting a "least publishable unit" strategy in which the smallest possible increments of progress are published at frequent intervals (a highly undesirable mode of research that many faculty believe characterizes the reality of the tenure process at their institutions).

Some respondents to the CRA-CSTB survey did say that they ignored the tenure process and concentrated their work on what they thought was interesting, relevant, and important. On the whole, these individuals tended to be from very highly ranked schools.[10]   A sub-

---

[10] The "ranking" referred to in the text concerns a survey published in 1982 that ranked 58 university research doctorate programs in computer science according to their reputations in the field (National Research Council (NRC). 1982. *An Assessment of Research-Doctorate Programs in the United States: Mathematical and Physical Sciences.* National Academy Press, Washington, D.C.). This ranking is being revised by the NRC's Office of Scientific and Engineering Personnel, and the next publication of this list is expected in 1995.

stantial minority of respondents to the CRA-CSTB survey said that an impending tenure decision drove them to focus more on publishing work that was demonstrably recognizable as research rather than pursuing projects with long time horizons. Some quotations follow:

> Now that I have tenure, I feel more free to pursue research on systems that I want to do rather than more short-term projects which will lead quickly to a collection of publications. [associate professor at a smaller private university]

> The tenure pressure has forced me to explore less speculative areas. Since I cannot afford to expend a significant amount of energy in an area that "didn't pan out," I am forced to do low-risk work. This tends to reduce the potential benefit of the work. [assistant professor at a large public university]

> I now feel more free to address longer-term problems that may not yield publications as regularly but will, I believe, turn out to be of more lasting value. [associate professor at a smaller public university]

The T&P process also influenced the work of junior faculty in other ways. For example, a substantial number indicated that the realities of the T&P process at their institutions drove them to do work that was more theoretical in nature than they would have preferred, simply because experimental work in their environment was not as highly valued. In most cases, this issue arose because the T&P process placed the greatest weight on journal publications in its evaluation of research, journal publications that are themselves biased away from experimental work. Survey respondents commented:

> I am coming up for tenure this year. It has already affected me in a big way because some of my most time-consuming activities in building actual systems do not produce sufficient publications per level of work, and so I expect to rely on some of my more theoretical work, which has indeed produced publications more easily. It is like a split personality, . . . what I consider my most substantial contributions are likely to be ignored, and I may earn tenure on more conventional work. [assistant professor at a smaller private university]

> I have tenure, but did primarily theoretical research before that. It was obvious from day one that systems building and getting tenure were not going to mix very well. Since receiving tenure, I have concentrated more on systems-oriented work, and indeed I have not published as many pages of material. Systems building has been part of the reason for this (there is not enough time to build systems, write as many papers as theoretical researchers, etc.). But I have also changed my idea of what is publishable, and [now] insist on having a real contribution before trying to publish something. [associate professor at a large public university]

In conclusion, it would seem to be in the scholar's, as well as the discipline's, best interest for everyone to work on his or her highest-priority problems. In the presence of tenure pressure, care must be taken to identify the risks and minimize them. A mentor (see Chapter 5) can provide the benefits of experience and can guide in the application of this generalized information to a junior faculty member's specific situation. Although the intellectual risks inherent in research problems will remain, much can be done to reduce methodological risks. In any event, there will not be enough time before the tenure decision. Yet a few papers in respected conferences documenting progress toward solving an important experimental problem represent a better accomplishment than a mountain of irrelevant paper.

## A NOTE ON OTHER DISCIPLINES

The issues faced by academic experimentalists in ECSE have partial analogues in other disciplines. For example, artists, performing musicians, and dramatists generate work products (sculptures, musical performances, plays) that are analogous to the artifacts of ECSE. However, in these fields, the standard for intellectual accomplishment includes both scholarly analysis or publication and "artistic creativity," a standard that—although subjective—is nevertheless amenable to peer review.[11] Universities seeking to evaluate the work of faculty artists, musicians, and dramatists consider the venues in which the works of these individuals are displayed (e.g., an exhibition at a major gallery is worth much more than one at the local community center), peer reviews of these works, and the stature of those peers. In addition, potential letter writers are generally given copies of the portfolio to the extent that it can be reproduced.

Engineers in noncomputer fields also produce artifacts that are judged on the basis of their utility to substantial audiences. However, as a broad generalization, it can be said that these artifacts are often based on a well-accepted theoretical foundation. An aeronautical engineer may design a system to control the flight of an airplane under particular circumstances (e.g., strong wind shear), and the flight control system will eventually be evaluated on the basis of its utility

---

[11] A document that describes the evaluation of intellectual contributions of faculty in the arts is *The Work of Arts Faculties in Higher Education,* a report assembled by the Landscape Architectural Accreditation Board, National Architectural Accrediting Board, and the National Associations of Schools of Art and Design, Dance, Music, and Theater. This report is undated.

in preventing crashes due to wind shear. However, control theory is a well-established and well-codified body of knowledge that enjoys paradigmatic status among control engineers. Thus, the aeronautical engineer is also likely to leave a "paper trail" on the way to implementing the flight control system.

## SUMMARY

In conducting ECSE research, faculty members will imagine new computing ideas, create artifacts to implement them, and measure properties of the artifacts. It is important that the artifacts work and equally important that they be made available.

The research may be of high quality by the goals, standards, and traditions of ECSE, yet not accord with the expectations of a theoretician or the "usual academic publish-or-perish" standards. However, experimentalists hired to a faculty deserve to be evaluated by the criteria of their chosen specialty. Accommodation may be necessary.

The committee believes that at the point a tenure decision is made, an experimentalist may have

- Fewer publications;
- Predominately conference publications;
- Nonstandard forms of dissemination, such as software; and
- No graduate students completed

and still be a truly spectacular researcher. A positive judgment should be made on the presence or absence of the following:

- One or more computational impact-producing artifacts completed;
- Research results disseminated to and used by the community;
- A reputation for novel systems solutions or ingenious experiments; and
- A filled or filling pipeline of well-trained graduate students.

It is the responsibility of the candidate to achieve distinction. It is the responsibility of the department and institution to recognize and reward it.

As a final thought, the committee emphasizes the consequences of two points developed in this chapter. It takes a long time to produce artifacts, and there are often long delays before the impact of an artifact can be determined. Given that the probationary period is brief in relation to the length of this process, it often happens that universities must "gamble" on promoting a promising assistant professor because the data to support the case are not definitive. Although this happens from time to time in all disciplines, it happens so often in ECSE that it may be the norm. There are examples of spectacular successes and unfortunate mistakes. Because a conservative strategy is not likely to succeed in the long run, universities are encouraged to seek the widest possible input into the promotion decision in order to increase their confidence in the decision.

# 5

# A Positive Environment for Academic ECSE

Previous chapters have discussed infrastructure, research evaluation, and educational issues as they relate to experimental computer scientists and engineers in academia. The committee intends this chapter to be a description of the characteristics of a positive academic environment in which experimental computer science and engineering (ECSE) can flourish, rather than criticism of any individual department. Recognizing that ECSE is thriving in some departments, but not in others, the committee expressly chose this formulation as a means of encapsulating those characteristics that seem to work well.

## MENTORING AND ADVOCACY

When Odysseus set out for Troy, he entrusted the care of his household to Mentor. Although the burden to succeed properly belongs to the researcher, young researchers setting out on their academic careers still need mentors, loyal friends, wise advisers, teachers, faithful counselors, guardians, and advocates to help advance their interests. Young experimentalists often face greater and more complicated demands than do their theoretically inclined colleagues, many of which follow from the project-oriented nature of the work.

## Mentoring

Recognizing these differences, computer science and engineering departments need to be proactive in helping to establish mentoring and advocacy relationships between junior and senior faculty members. (As used here, *mentoring* refers to advice from a senior faculty member to a junior faculty member. *Advocacy* refers to commentary, input, and argument from a senior faculty member to department chairs, deans, and others higher up in the university hierarchy in arguing for and promoting the interests of a junior faculty member.)

These arrangements should be made openly and explicitly. Young faculty should know from the start whom to consult for advice and counseling. They will appreciate the help and attention, and the department will have created a positive factor in retaining and recruiting first-rate faculty. The senior faculty members who take on mentoring and advocacy roles should be encouraged to meet, discuss their situations, and find ways to support each other. The more general types of guidance are listed below, and Box 5.1 describes specific mentoring tasks.

Given the time and resource demands of ECSE, a junior faculty member must "hit the ground running" to be successful. In all but the most unusual cases, the process is bootstrapped: early research success using start-up resources and no graduate students is parlayed into funding that can support a more ambitious implementation effort with graduate students who should by then be trained. The more ambitious artifact must be completed in time to perform the experiments so that the results can be disseminated to the community early enough for the work to be evaluated by the tenure letter writers.

Senior faculty mentors have an important role in facilitating such an outcome. In addition to technical assistance, senior faculty can provide advice about practical aspects of experimental work, such as managing time, money, and space. They can also provide guidance about the expectations for tenure. Following are several areas in which mentoring senior faculty can play important roles:

- *Establishing cooperative and collaborative environments.* Since junior faculty generally lack reputations that attract resources, they are often dependent on senior faculty to obtain entry to established laboratories that can provide needed equipment, staff, and technical skills, as well as an intellectual community. Junior faculty without funding of their own can participate in existing grants while seeking independent sources of funding. New projects that start surrounded by established activities enjoy an increased likelihood of success.

## BOX 5.1  A Mentoring Checklist

### Publication

In which journals and conferences should the junior faculty member publish? How often? Can the mentor review papers before submission for publication?

### Funding

Which funding agencies support the type of work the junior faculty member wants to do? Which industrial companies share the junior faculty member's intellectual interests? Who within agencies and companies are the right people to meet? To what extent are university start-up funds adequate for a new junior faculty member's initial work? Can the mentor review the junior faculty member's grant proposals?

### Collaboration

What senior people in the field share intellectual interests with the junior faculty member? Who has laboratories or other resources that are shareable with the junior faculty member?

### Visibility

Who are the senior people in the field who should know the junior faculty member's work? How can seminars or other presentation forums be arranged to showcase the junior faculty member's work? What contributions has the junior faculty member made that are not widely recognized?

### Problem Choice

What problems should the junior faculty member choose that are doable in the given academic environment *and* have the potential for substantial impact on the field? How can a research program be structured so that it has meaningful intermediate outputs? What are dead-end problems that should be avoided? Is the project consistent with the resources that will be available?

### Students and Teaching

How can good and appropriate students be attracted to work with junior faculty? How can the junior faculty member's teaching be improved? At what point is the junior faculty member spending too much time on teaching and education?

---

**Service**

What service activities should the junior faculty member perform or avoid? How can the junior faculty member be protected from inappropriate service work?

**Logistics**

What vendors should supply the junior faculty member's equipment or software? Who in the university should be approached about obtaining laboratory space?

---

- *Matching project scale and scope to available resources.* Because they lack experience in research management, junior faculty are often unable to assess the appropriate scale of a project relative to their operating environment. In their enthusiasm, junior faculty members may embark on projects that are too large or complex given the resources likely to be available. Senior faculty can give advice about what is reasonable given the limits of available resources. Later, as an advocate to the department and the university, the mentor may be called on to explain how the young researcher's accomplishments are consonant with the resources at hand.
- *Improving the visibility of protégés.* Senior faculty can play a key role in generating speaking opportunities for junior faculty at departmental colloquia, industrial research laboratories, or other universities, workshops, and other settings in which the junior faculty member's work can be showcased. Perhaps more importantly, they can also encourage junior faculty to make such presentations.
- *Recognizing collaborative contributions.* The collaborative nature of many ECSE research projects is often at odds with the need of the tenure and promotion (T&P) process to identify contributions made by specific individuals. Such identification may be particularly important in the case of an individual who makes intellectually substantive contributions to an unsuccessful project that failed for entirely separate reasons. Given that collaborative research projects are most often carried out under the direction of a senior faculty member, junior faculty collaborators may not be recognized publicly for their specific contributions without explicit acknowledgment and promotion of their efforts by the senior project director.
- *Counseling protégés to adopt research strategies that produce significant intermediate results.* Even in acknowledging the fact that ECSE research may involve "all-or-nothing" risks, researchers are still best

advised to avoid mega-projects that after years of producing nothing emit a single, definitive magnum opus. A more conservative approach, which often requires the guidance of an experienced researcher, is to structure the study so that it produces intermediate results suitable for publication, thereby balancing significance and scope against the need for visible output. Examples might include reporting results from simulations used in designing the artifact, describing technology used to build the artifact, or presenting analytical studies of some aspect of the artifact. Intermediate publications serve as concrete evidence of research progress. Additionally, they provide early exposure of the ideas to the community that can result in prompt feedback useful for midcourse corrections.

As the discussion above suggests, a mentor must be intimately familiar with the ECSE field, research practices, and community. It is important for mentors to understand the career and research goals of their ostensible protégés. The senior faculty have to take responsibility for becoming familiar with the peer groups, conferences, and organizations that are important to a young researcher's career. Well-meaning though a senior theoretician may be, the mentoring role for a junior experimentalist is best served by a senior experimentalist.

A department that does not have appropriate senior experimental faculty to serve as mentors for junior faculty should consider finding someone at another university or laboratory who can play the role of outside adviser, perhaps by using regular visits (at least once or twice a year), telephone calls, and e-mail to maintain frequent contact with the young faculty. (A new faculty member's doctoral adviser is ideally situated to play such a role.) External mentors can play the same sort of role that visiting committees play during the evaluation of departments—providing advice, offering contacts, and being a sounding board for new ideas. This is also a way for universities without large, established experimental programs to develop such programs.

## Advocacy

Although the roles of advocates and mentors overlap, they are somewhat different. Whereas a mentor gives advice and counsel and guides the junior faculty member through the academic jungle, an advocate is distinctly partisan. The advocate's job is to advance the interests of junior faculty members and to help them make the best possible case for their promotion.

Perhaps the most important role of an advocate is laying the groundwork for a tenure case within the university. University-wide (or

---

## BOX 5.2 An Advocate's Checklist

The functions of an advocate in the tenure and promotion process include:

- Helping to select or nominate specific letter writers familiar with the candidate's work (including collaborators), based on their ability to evaluate such work;
- Explaining and documenting key characteristics of ECSE to those outside the field, pointing out potential mismatches between ECSE and more traditional disciplines;
- Accumulating evidence of impact of the junior faculty member's work on practice, including letters from industrial contacts, and arguing the case that industrial scientists are well-placed to judge impact;
- Obtaining letters from other researchers who may have used parts of the experiments in their own work, or who may have used the experimental results to guide their work;
- Soliciting referee reports from conferences to document the quality of conference contributions;
- Documenting how negative experimental results may have helped drive the field in a positive way;
- Explaining the structure and pecking order of the literature; knowing which conferences and journals are respected, prestigious, and well refereed; being knowledgeable about acceptance rates and review procedures for conferences and private journals in which the junior faculty member has made presentations or published;
- Explaining the significance of artifacts produced by the junior faculty member;
- Understanding historical matches between resources and project scale;
- Explaining the importance of collaborative work in ECSE; and
- Extrapolating the future performance of the junior faculty member.

---

even school-wide) T&P committees may not understand the nature of ECSE very well and may attempt to judge tenure candidates according to inappropriate criteria. Accordingly, an effective advocate has to know the field well—its standards, its interesting questions, its history, its characteristic work modes—and be able to communicate the goals and aspirations of ECSE as a discipline to others. Box 5.2 describes some of the things that advocates may have to do to support the tenure case of a junior faculty member.

A forceful and experienced advocate may be particularly important in those universities that have not institutionally recognized the significance of artifacts in scholarly endeavors. At these universities, an advocate may have to argue anew for every ECSE promotion or tenure case that the creation of artifacts can be a legitimate focus of scholarly research.

## DESIDERATA FOR THE TENURE AND PROMOTION PROCESS

Universities evaluating candidates for tenure or promotion take into account a number of indicators. The committee recognizes a wide range of approaches to evaluating candidates for tenure and promotion, and it does not wish to intrude on institutional prerogatives in determining how best to evaluate candidates. At the same time, the committee believes that evaluators should use standards and criteria that normally characterize productive work in the ECSE discipline, rather than standards that may be applicable to more traditional academic disciplines. Care should be taken not to exclude meaningful evidence of achievement simply because it is nonstandard. Indeed, the committee believes that T&P committees and university administrators should take a catholic perspective on the available evidence, regardless of the different forms in which such evidence appears.

The purpose of the discussion below is to point out how characteristics of the ECSE discipline may affect the indicators that universities take into account in making T&P decisions and how those indicators should be evaluated. However, it is clearly the prerogative of individual universities to determine the relative weight that each indicator should carry for T&P candidates. The committee observes that some institutions, notably those with a strong and continuing tradition of experimental work, already take these characteristics into account in their T&P processes.

### Publications

Many universities regard archival journal and book publications as the primary medium in which scholarly work is demonstrated, whereas "mere" presentations at professional meetings are regarded as second-rate. Although such practices are not the rule at universities with strong experimental traditions, anecdotal evidence suggests that they are considerably more common in universities without such traditions.

As noted in Chapter 4, publications in ECSE take a variety of forms: technical reports, conference proceedings, or articles in archival journals. For ECSE, publication in certain conference proceedings may carry as much or more weight than publication in highly regarded journals. The dilemma of choosing between the requirements for the "proper form" of an academic record and the "content" for ECSE was nicely stated by an assistant professor at a major private university in response to the CRA-CSTB survey:

> Tenure means that I have to spend an enormous amount of time writing papers for archival journals and conferences, so that people can peer-review me without understanding what I do. Most of the impact of [experimental] research work comes from dissemination channels such as e-mail, via which the software artifacts produced by the research can be spread into the community.

Given this tension, candidates for promotion in ECSE may face a significant disadvantage compared to their more theoretically inclined colleagues. Specifically, their publication portfolios may well be shorter (because of the time-consuming nature of ECSE research) and may contain fewer publications in archival journals (because of the field's preference for the timeliness of conference publication). Such characteristics should not prejudice a candidate's case, if it is documented in other ways that important and recognized intellectual output has been produced (e.g., through the production of significant computing artifacts, as described below).

ECSE articles in archival journals can be expected primarily at the end of a project, independent of whether the experiment was a success or failure. Such articles distill project results and summarize the issues raised, the insights gained, and the implications for future research. They unify the results of the project and describe how it fits within the larger context of the field. Accordingly, it is not uncommon to find a single archival journal publication for an entire multiyear project.

By contrast, conference publications relate work in progress and intermediate milestones. A typical project may result in several conference publications but only one journal publication. Technical reports complement both conference and journal publications by describing the project in substantial detail; such reports are an essential vehicle for disseminating the specifics of the project.

The timing of journal publications as it relates to the nature of the discipline should also be recognized. It is not uncommon for a T&P committee to interpret an unevenly distributed publication record (e.g., a long gap with no publications followed by a "surge" of publications near the tenure decision) as a response to the tenure decision rather than as an indication of true productivity. In the case of experimentalists, this interpretation should be examined carefully, because the time scales of project completion are often comparable to the probationary period. T&P committees might wish to examine the extent to which the publications taken together indicate a coherent intellectual theme. If so, a publication surge is less suspect than if the publications are relatively disconnected.

Faculties, deans, and university administrators generally disclaim in public assertions that simplistic methods such as publication counting are used in considering candidates for tenure. Whether or not such methods are used at any given university is difficult to determine, although there is a widespread perception that publication counting is widely practiced. It would not be surprising if it were practiced at many universities, because the appropriate basis for a promotion decision—significance and impact of research—is difficult to verify independently by committees far removed from the candidate's research specialty.

In short, a candidate's record of publication in archival journals is only one aspect of the individual's overall portfolio, and for ECSE perhaps a misleading one at that. The candidate's record in producing innovative and useful artifacts of high quality and the letters of recommendation supporting the promotion may be better indicators of his or her history and likely future performance.

In any event, publication portfolios should include documentation regarding matters such as frequency of publication, acceptance rates, and publishing history for journal or conference publications, as well as the board of editors or program committee members. These can help evaluation committees to understand the basis used to determine the worthiness of those publications.

### Artifacts

A track record that might appear modest when assessed by counting journal articles may in fact be truly spectacular when evaluated in the context of a discipline in which a technical reputation is founded as much on functional artifacts as it is on publications. Production of artifacts is so important to the field that a standard part of *any* experimentalist's curriculum vitae should be a section describing computing artifacts produced by the experimentalist.

However, the reality in many universities—especially those without strong engineering traditions—is that artifacts are mentioned only in the context of such "creative fields" as music, art, and theater; evaluations are conducted on the basis of the quality of the artistic production and make use of evidence such as published reviews of performances or awards in juried exhibitions. Thus, the importance of artifacts to ECSE research may need to be clearly established as a principle. Once the principle has been established, the focus should turn to the impact of the artifacts that the candidate has produced. One obvious dimension is intellectual impact—to what extent has an artifact had an impact on researchers in the field? This question is treated in depth in Chapter 1.

However, another dimension of impact—impact on practice—is, in the committee's view, underappreciated. An ECSE researcher who creates an innovative computing artifact whose primary impact has been on practice (e.g., an artifact that is embodied in a large number of nonresearch systems or used by a large number of "just plain users") has made a substantive and meaningful contribution in the tradition of ECSE, similar to that of a theoretician who proves an important lemma. Of course, simplistic measures such as "number of users to whom the artifact has been disseminated" or "number of FTP downloads of software from the researcher's laboratory" are as meaningless as publication counts. The true impact of an artifact is documented more meaningfully by letters from prominent and trustworthy colleagues in academia or industry, and any other users of the artifact.

In addition, the scale of the project that produces any given artifact should be an important consideration in its evaluation. Specifically, it is inappropriate to expect a small-scale experimental project (e.g., one on the order of $100,000) to produce results that are comparable to those attained by projects 10 times that size.

## Review Letters

Letters that evaluate the accomplishments and the promise of candidates for promotion (especially at the point of tenure) are an integral part of the candidate's portfolio. Indeed, for academicians in ECSE, as in other disciplines, letters may be the most important component of the portfolio. The primary reason is simple: impact on and value to others are the key qualities to be established in an individual's work. Honest and well-documented letters by knowledgeable evaluators are the best way to demonstrate impact and testify to value. A secondary reason is that letters expressing the judgment of senior researchers may be necessary to identify ideas or artifacts with large but as-yet unrealized *potential* for impact.[1]

---

[1] The long time scales required for artifact implementation may well mean that a good idea does not have time to diffuse into the community at large during the first six years of an assistant professor's career. Moreover, the difference between a project that demonstrates the technical feasibility of a promising concept and one that develops the proof-of-concept prototype to releasable form may be a factor of 10 in resources spent, even if no new ideas emerge as those additional resources are spent. In other cases, a useful innovation may be part of a larger system that will be deployed in the future, thus restricting experience with the actual implementation.

It is important that letter writers be provided with enough information to make valid and useful judgments, such as copies of the papers highlighted by the candidate in the publication section of the curriculum vitae and obviously a copy of the curriculum vitae itself. The reviewer should make explicit comparisons with other faculty members in the candidate's peer group.

Given the importance of letters, the selection of letter writers becomes a critical problem. The committee believes that *the primary criteria in selecting potential letter writers should be their stature in the field and their familiarity with the candidate's work.* Other factors, such as the letter writer's institutional location or status as a research collaborator of the candidate, should not be reasons for eschewing letters from such individuals. Of course, good arguments can be made to support the proposition that letter writers should not consist *exclusively* of collaborators or industrial scientists because of potential bias, unfamiliarity with the academic environment, and so on. However, to exclude letters from such individuals or to impose arbitrary limits on these letters is as inappropriate as including only letters written by senior academics who have no personal knowledge of the candidate's work.

It is particularly important that letters from individuals in industry not be limited arbitrarily; such letters should carry a weight equal to those of similarly qualified and reputable individuals in academia. The reason is that ECSE work with high impact is likely to affect industry. Much of the most advanced work in ECSE is done in industry, and many of the top researchers in ECSE are found there. (Analogous remarks apply to qualified and reputable ECSE researchers at government laboratories.) Similarly, the potential evaluator's reputation within the field, and his or her knowledge of the candidate's work, are far more important than the overall reputation of the evaluator's home institution. Although this proposition may seem obvious, the committee found many examples of universities in which review letters from industry scientists and engineers are not only discouraged but often never sought.

As for collaborators, the concern that they may be unduly biased toward (or, on occasion, against) the candidate on the basis of existing personal relationship is a valid one. However, to avoid letters from collaborators in a field as intrinsically collaborative as ECSE is to eliminate some of the best possible input regarding the candidate's intellectual capacity, creativity, and originality. Documenting the extent and nature of an individual's contributions is surely required. The best way to find out, of course, is to ask the principals and read their letters with care. Attempts to allocate specific percentages of credit to individuals for collaborative work are foolish in the extreme.

## Funding History

Tenure and promotion committees often take into account the candidate's track record in obtaining research funding, on the assumption that the ability to attract outside funding is an indicator of competence. Often, faculty members are evaluated on the aggressiveness with which they have sought out available research opportunities and how effectively they have met the expectations of funding agencies.

Most ECSE researchers do require considerable funding in order to pursue their research; the only exceptions are those instances in which the faculty member is fortunate enough to make connections with an existing laboratory and experimental infrastructure or those in which the faculty member has been able to develop an experimental research program "on the cheap."

Although funding is an enabling factor for ECSE research, it is not in itself necessarily demonstrative of intellectual achievement. Indeed, a faculty member who has structured his or her research to produce meaningful results, with high impact, on a limited budget deserves praise for creativity and good problem selection, rather than censure for not producing dollars for the university.

Government funding decisions—even at strongly peer-reviewed agencies such as the National Science Foundation—are not (and should not be) based simply on a rank ordering of proposal quality and a cutoff above some specified line. Although reviewer scores of proposals could be used to generate a rank ordering of those proposals, program directors are expected to take other considerations into account. "Hot" topics wax and wane, and reviewer scores tend to trail the curve—so some topics are often scored higher simply because the reviewers are more familiar with them. One job of a good program director is to identify new topics that could extend the frontiers of the field in novel directions, which sometimes means funding proposals in new areas that may not have received particularly good scores. A second job of program directors is to maintain a good balance of topics in their portfolios—so slightly poorer proposals in an emerging area ought to be chosen ahead of slightly better ones in oversubscribed areas. In short, program directors who do their jobs well may not be funding only the highly meritorious proposals. Consequently, a paucity of research funding should not be held against the junior faculty member who has otherwise demonstrated an adequate level of significant research productivity.

As noted above, industry can be an important source for the funding of ECSE research. Industry funds can support equipment grants, fellowships for students, small cash grants, and major cooperative efforts. In many cases, especially with equipment grants, industry decisions seem more likely to be made on the basis of the reputation of the school than of the individual. Nevertheless, individuals deserve credit for receiving this kind of support.

Cooperative research and development grants are sometimes problematic, because much of the work may be done at the company and relatively little money given to the university. Therefore, what may look like a minor project on the résumé may actually constitute a significant achievement with major impact. Reviewing industrial grants is normally done strictly within a company, but obtaining such a grant is generally a reliable indication of impact when a long-term relation can be established.

## Other Considerations in the T&P Process

### Ph.D. Students

Given the nationwide average of 6.4 years for students to complete Ph.D. degrees, it is unrealistic to expect a junior ECSE faculty member to produce very many Ph.D. students before a tenure decision must be made; he or she may be fortunate to have graduated one, especially if a research laboratory and team had to be built from scratch. However, it is not unreasonable to expect an assistant professor at this time to have a number of students in the pipeline and one or more close to graduation.

More important than the number of graduated Ph.D. students at this stage is their intellectual and professional development. Relevant indicators may include their production of useful and novel artifacts (even if small scale), their intellectual independence, and even their records of public presentations of work. Moreover, because incoming graduate students may tend to avoid junior faculty in favor of senior faculty with established reputations, such assessment should also take note of the quality of the students available to the junior faculty member.

### Consulting

Consulting can be an indicator of the research impact of a candidate's work. However, a full description of consulting work (including products that have been or may be developed under the consulting arrangement) is necessary for T&P committees to judge this impact.

Nondisclosure agreements are thus particularly problematic for junior faculty members. Given the tradition of academic research as work that may be freely published and disseminated, consultants whose primary allegiances are to academia are urged to resist restrictive nondisclosure agreements to the maximum extent possible. Consulting relationships that focus on implementation at the expense of reportable scholarly work may remunerate the faculty member/consultant but do not advance the research enterprise. Instead, faculty members should seek consulting relationships that strengthen or enhance their own research programs or that provide opportunities, such as scholarly publication, in which they can obtain public recognition for their work. For example, faculty members may be able to negotiate short and finite periods of time in which they will refrain from discussing their work in public, or they may agree that technical details should be kept private but conceptual ideas can be freely discussed. Patent applications might be considered. However, in the absence of such expressions of understanding, faculty members who undertake proprietary consulting work do so at their own risk with respect to the T&P process.

A second potentially negative aspect of consulting should be considered as well. Given the financial rewards available from consulting for industry, ECSE faculty, especially those with tenure, have great incentives to undertake such activities. If too much time is spent on consulting activities, the perception of a less-than-dedicated "part-timer" occupying a full-time faculty slot may take hold. Such perceptions may be rather negative, especially in publicly funded institutions whose legislatures may already be concerned about "faculty who spend so little time teaching."

Still, despite the potential pitfalls, consulting for industry can carry a variety of benefits for faculty members entirely apart from the remuneration involved. It can familiarize them with the problems facing industry, thereby suggesting potentially interesting research directions. It can help to place a faculty member's teaching in a better context, especially for students who will eventually work in industry (see discussion on teaching below). Finally, it can be the basis for acquiring additional research funding.

### Workshops

Workshops are specialized conferences with a focused theme. In many cases, participation is by invitation only; in other cases, the program committee selects from extended abstracts submitted by researchers in the area. Workshops play an important role in setting research directions in a given area and the timely exchange of ideas.

In this way, they can be superior to conferences in other fields. Participation in workshops can demonstrate community acceptance of a researcher's competence if not the researcher's work per se.

## Teaching[2]

The rapid changes in the technological substrate of ECSE mean that even lower-division ECSE courses will need frequent updating, much more so than courses (e.g., in the physical sciences) in which the fundamentals remain the same from year to year. In addition, recent reports such as *Computing the Future* have called for the development of interdisciplinary connections between computer science and other problem domains, and the development and teaching of interdisciplinary courses would be evidence that the individuals involved were furthering the interests of the field.

Rapid change affects the core curriculum of CS&E even at the graduate level. This provides significant opportunities for junior faculty to develop new courses in or near the area of their research—opportunities that may be less available in more established science and engineering disciplines such as physics, whose core courses tend to change much more slowly. At the same time, exploiting such

---

[2] The relatively brief discussion of teaching in this section should not be taken to imply a committee judgment about the relative importance of teaching versus research. The issues raised in this section are issues that are characteristic of ECSE vis-à-vis other disciplines, but the much broader question of the appropriate balance between teaching and research is outside the scope of this report, as are questions such as, How much credit should a candidate for tenure or promotion receive for the writing of a textbook versus obtaining excellent student evaluations?

Nevertheless, a number of the faculty who responded to the CRA-CSTB survey made spontaneous comments regarding the teaching-research balance. Here are two:

> I find that the pressure to publish and get money detracts from the undergraduates. They are often short-changed, and I believe that the situation cannot continue. The nation as a whole is not being served well, if the only people who get tenure are those who have little interest in teaching undergraduates. Is our nation's policy of ignoring undergraduates a significant reason why the majority of our graduate students come from overseas?

> Keep your teaching and administrative responsibilities in perspective— if your research suffers too much, then you won't get tenure. Do a reasonable job at teaching and do carry out essential administrative chores, and most importantly be sensitive to your [own] students' needs, but remember this: there is no end to the distractions that will keep you from doing your research and writing those papers. You will have to say no at times when you would rather not, but if you don't learn how to say no when it's necessary (and to do so nicely), then your life will become very, very difficult.

opportunities is often very time-consuming for junior ECSE faculty, because there is often no suitable textbook even for core courses in ECSE. Advocates for junior faculty will want to ensure that the significance of such course development does not go unnoticed at promotion time.

The competent supervision of undergraduate research in ECSE is a notable accomplishment in a teaching portfolio, especially given the difficulties in formulating a meaningful ECSE research problem that an undergraduate can plausibly undertake. Undergraduate papers or presentations reporting research results would be a powerful indicator of such supervision.

Teaching has an industrial dimension as well. Terms such as *partnerships with industry* have entered the vocabulary of computer science departments' strategic plans. Innovative courses are being developed that use the arena of experimental computer science to bring industry into tighter contact with academic education. Documentation might include work toward establishing industrial advisory boards and direct consulting with industry to develop specialized courses for industry or new regular courses in the undergraduate curriculum.

## Service

Although faculty in all disciplines have service responsibilities, those in ECSE have two special challenges. The first is that ECSE faculty may be asked to provide service to the university by developing, maintaining, or upgrading software to be used by other members of the university community not in the faculty member's immediate sphere of research interest. In other cases, ECSE faculty are asked to serve on numerous committees to solve computer-related problems faced by the university. Networking experts find themselves on task forces to develop an appropriate networking infrastructure for the campus. Database experts are asked to serve on committees to help solve registration problems, and any ECSE faculty member might be appointed to a committee to select the best system for automating the library.

In general, the committee believes that administrations should be discouraged from asking junior ECSE faculty to perform such roles *in addition* to the demands for committee service placed on all faculty members. However, such service may be appropriate when the overall service load to the university for ECSE faculty (including such computer-related work) is commensurate with that of faculty in other disciplines.

The second special challenge results from service at the national level. Service includes participation in standards committees, service on advisory boards, invitations to serve on national task forces (including committees of the Computer Science and Telecommunications Board) to solve specific problems in computer science, service to computer societies, and service as reviewers of publications and grant proposals. ECSE has far fewer faculty than older scientific disciplines such as physics or chemistry, and the demands made on senior ECSE faculty for national service are substantial.

## INSTITUTIONAL CONTRIBUTIONS
## TO THE ENVIRONMENT

In addition to orchestrating a supportive intellectual environment for ECSE and evaluating ECSE faculty in accordance with the standards that characterize the field, departments and universities are directly responsible for certain other aspects of the environment:

• *Start-up funding.* As noted earlier, beginning assistant professors are rarely able to secure outside funding in their first year. In other experimental sciences, even new assistant professors are often provided with a start-up package when hired that includes a laboratory, equipment, and other resources. Many universities with ECSE programs do not offer start-up packages at all or, at best, offer incoming faculty (both theoretical and experimental) a single workstation.

A start-up package should be offered to beginning assistant professors that is large enough to begin research immediately. At the least, start-up packages for junior ECSE faculty should, when justified by the needs of the research that is planned, be comparable in total dollar value to those offered incoming junior faculty in the more traditional laboratory sciences.

• *Commitment of resources.* Departments must understand that high-quality ECSE research with a great impact often demands a substantial commitment of resources. In particular, they must pay careful attention to the following:

• Equipment upgrades, which for state-of-the-art systems may be necessary as often as yearly;
• Equipment maintenance;
• Laboratory space;
• Technical staff, to keep the computing environment current;
• Software resources such as computer-aided design (CAD) tools; and
• Hardware resources such as networking and servers.

- *Intellectual property issues.* Given the intimate connection between ECSE researchers in academia and industry, departments and universities should promote these interactions. However, one of the most time-consuming aspects of developing these relationships is the resolution of matters related to potential intellectual property arrangements with industrially supported research, or research undertaken jointly with industry. All too often, a faculty researcher lines up an industrial partner, only to see the actual start of research delayed by many months while the university's lawyers negotiate with the company in question. A standard policy or prenegotiated umbrella agreements would go a long way toward facilitating academic-industrial research cooperation.[3]

- *Teaching assistant support.* As noted earlier, grading and the maintenance of equipment and software place great time demands on ECSE faculty teaching time-intensive, laboratory-based courses. Adequate teaching assistant support for these courses is necessary if the faculty member is to maintain a full portfolio of professional activities.

- *Teaching assignments.* Faculty starting a new ECSE research program will need to build teams to carry out the work. Departments can help by providing opportunities for such faculty members to teach advanced seminars in which graduate students can receive needed training in preparation for joining a research project.

---

[3] At universities inexperienced in dealing with licensing and patenting activities, the potentially profitable research activities of ECSE faculty may generate conflict between the faculty and the university administration. As one faculty member put it,

> Not only are experimentalists subject to undue pressure to get funding, but they are also the subject of university desire to raise funding through commercial ventures. Technology produced by experimentalists is often the subject matter of patenting and licensing activities. This opens a whole new realm of "back-door university politics" that is unpleasant at best. Universities have yet to learn how to treat and deal with their faculty that produce valuable artifacts.

# 6

# Special Needs and Concerns of Non-Doctorate-Granting and Less Recognized Institutions

To this point the discussion has focused on the situation of experimental computer scientists and engineers at research-oriented academic institutions with doctoral programs, the Forsythe list schools. Yet institutions without doctoral programs face many of the same problems. Moreover, factors such as size, faculty mix, history, and resource availability can further complicate the matter of career advancement for faculty at schools without doctoral programs. The opportunities and problems of non-doctorate-granting (NPhD) institutions are considered in this chapter.

Chapter 1 argues that the reasons for conducting experimental computer science and engineering research (ECSE) at universities include keeping the faculty on the cutting edge of this fast-moving field, maintaining the vitality of curricula in a technologically sensitive area, and keeping course work exciting by enabling faculty to draw on state-of-the-art examples and exercises from their research domains. These benefits are at least as critical for the NPhD schools, with their greater emphasis on teaching, as for Ph.D.-granting institutions. Accordingly, it is advantageous to use research experience as a means of achieving and maintaining high technical value and relevance.

NPhD schools vary: they include four-year colleges, universities with master's but not Ph.D. programs, and to a lesser extent, Ph.D.-granting institutions that graduate very small numbers of Ph.D. students every year. However, they share one crucial characteristic: they do not have a long-established research tradition, and many such institutions have only recently enlarged their missions to include "research" to any substantial degree. This lack of a research tradition is an example of a problem that Ph.D.-granting institutions do not have, but that manifests itself, for example, in evaluating faculty for promotion at NPhD schools. This and other problems of NPhD schools can be grouped by their common features into three categories: mission, size, and resources. The issues covered here are also generally applicable to universities that have recently established Ph.D. programs.

## MISSION

The NPhD school's goal of having faculty actively engaged in research has several consequences for the faculty, especially for those in ECSE. Chief among these is the substantial teaching load that is characteristic of NPhD institutions. Teaching is a time-consuming activity. When it is done right—and it must be done right, because quality teaching is often the selling point of NPhD schools—there is little time for research. This is a critical problem for ECSE faculty, given the large investment of time and intellectual resources required to create or experiment with an artifact. No school can, in fairness, expect significant research from ECSE faculty in the presence of extensive teaching obligations.

The mission of NPhD schools implies a second serious consequence for ECSE research: the absence of doctoral students. As noted in Chapter 2, Ph.D. graduate students are essential to creating artifacts, the medium in which ECSE research is conducted. By definition, there are no doctoral students at NPhD schools. The alternative is to engage advanced undergraduates and master's degree students in constructing artifacts, but the nature of their participation will differ from that of doctoral students. First, they must be closely supervised, a characteristic that is consonant with the goals of NPhD schools. Second, the requirements of the task must be more completely specified because the student presumably has less background. Third, the magnitude of the task must be modest because the student's available time—both in duration and in hours per day—is typically more modest. Fourth, many master's students are not full-time students. Such considerations limit the artifacts that can be created and the experimentation that can be conducted.

A third aspect of the mission of NPhD schools that affects ECSE research concerns the ability to compete for grant funding. Both federal agencies and industry favor Ph.D.-granting institutions in research funding, and, to a large degree, NPhD schools are ill-prepared to compete for foundation funding because of the lack of administrative support for all aspects of the process.  Nevertheless, it seems to be in the interest of both industry and the federal government to provide research support.  As noted, the quality of the educational offering is greatly enhanced.  Industry should take note of the fact that its laudable policy of donating equipment for teaching at NPhD schools can probably be greatly leveraged by a modest additional offering of state-of-the-art equipment to the faculty for research.  A faculty member excited about the research he or she is doing on a company's computer will be a more effective teacher to the students using the company's teaching donations.

## SIZE

Most NPhD schools are smaller than the typical Ph.D.-granting institutions, and so computer science and engineering (CS&E) departments in NPhD schools have fewer faculty.  Indeed, to put the NPhD peer group's concerns into perspective with other parts of this report, it may be difficult to identify "experimental" or "theoretical" faculty members at NPhD schools.  This can be an asset—certain issues affecting the intellectual environment at Ph.D.-granting institutions are not relevant for NPhD schools—but it can also constrain members of the peer group.

One consequence of small size applicable to faculty who conduct experimental work is that there are few colleagues with whom to collaborate.  Given that collaboration is characteristic of much ECSE research, experimental work at NPhD schools must be formulated especially carefully.  If an artifact is to be created, it should be smaller in scale and narrower in range because of the smaller number of researchers available to bring expertise to the work.

A much less easily resolved consequence of small size is the lack of a suitable academic mentor.  Although there are certainly faculty on campus from whom a new assistant professor can receive guidance about teaching and other aspects of academic life, research guidance and direction may be unavailable.  As suggested for Ph.D.-granting institutions with no suitable experimental senior faculty member to act as a mentor, NPhD schools may be able to enlist a faculty member at another school to fill this role.  An optimal solution to both the lack-of-collaborator and the lack-of-mentor problems would be to promote extramural collaboration.

Finally, small size brings the reality of inadequate staff support.  Although this is partly a resource problem (see below), it has another implication. Because the staff inadequacies at NPhD schools are so severe, faculty are often called on to perform system administration and maintenance tasks for departments and teaching facilities that are performed by technical staff at Ph.D.-granting institutions. These tasks take valuable time that could be applied to research. NPhD school administrations must provide staff support if they expect meaningful research from their faculty. Staff support is as beneficial as a reduced teaching load in terms of allowing time for research. It also represents a more economic allocation of resources.

## RESOURCES

Budgets are tight at NPhD schools and resources are scarce, and it is unrealistic to set a goal of faculty research without providing the means to achieve it. Critical to conducting ECSE research, as noted throughout this report, is access to the Internet. The ECSE community is electronic, and faculty cannot realistically participate without being, literally, plugged in. The importance of Internet access is underscored by the fact that it is key to solving the collaboration and mentoring problems discussed above. Similarly, hardware, software, and laboratory space are necessary to support experimental research. Although successful researchers can perhaps be expected eventually to provide for much of their own equipment and software needs, researchers at NPhD schools need seed funding to create laboratory facilities and sustained support for maintenance, staff, and so on.

It is obvious that if ECSE relies almost exclusively on conferences as the means of rapid dissemination of information, it is essential for ECSE researchers to attend conferences. NPhD schools have especially limited travel budgets, which constrains the opportunity for experimentalists to travel. Nevertheless, if faculty members are to be effectively engaged in experimental research, they must make their accomplishments known, learn of the latest advances in their field, see demonstrations of proof-of-existence artifacts, and so on, at workshops and conferences.

## MODELS FOR CONDUCTING ECSE RESEARCH
## AT NPHD SCHOOLS

The smaller scale of ECSE research projects feasible at NPhD schools mitigates some of the problems noted elsewhere in this report (e.g., the need for extensive infrastructure); nevertheless, many problems remain. The key question is how to organize ECSE research in the NPhD context to maximize success.

## Proof-of-Performance Research

As already noted, the size and complexity of artifacts are constrained by the resources that can be invested in them—faculty time, student time, funding, equipment, infrastructure, and so on. Thus the first model for research at an NPhD school is not to build artifacts at all, but rather to concentrate on experimenting with existing artifacts (e.g., software that has been updated or hardware located at other sites and accessed remotely) or verifying the experimental claims of others. Enormous savings are realized by not having to create the original artifact.

Because the tradition in ECSE is to share, it is not difficult to acquire access to artifacts; research software can be copied by using FTPs, and the remote log-in capabilities of the Internet can be used to obtain access to research hardware located off-site. Once remote capabilities are available, experiments in the proof-of-performance research style are possible. Of course, the proper equipment will be needed to run them, but in many cases a scientific workstation suffices. Additionally, there may be a natural "research constituency" available to those using this approach. That is, other scientists, possibly including the artifact's creators, may be working in the area and share an interest in the results, thus forming a valuable technical peer group. Although such work might not be publishable as a full article or conference presentation, it might be appropriate for publication as a "technical correspondence."

## Collaborative Research

A second model for research by NPhD school faculty is to collaborate with faculty at Ph.D.-granting institutions. Such collaboration could take the form of contributing to the creation of, or experimentation with, a large artifact. The mechanism for initiating such collaboration is the personal relationship of the researchers involved. To launch the research properly may require the NPhD faculty member to visit the project, for example, during the summer. At project meetings the (often ill-specified) research strategy for creating the artifact can be established. Then, by using the Internet, telephone, fax, and other forms of communication, the project collaborators keep in contact during the academic year. Such arrangements are decidedly in the interest of all participants.

Computer science departments at NPhD schools should encourage faculty interested in experimentation to assess realistically how such research can be conducted under the prevailing conditions. At

Ph.D.-granting institutions, experimentalists should be encouraged to pursue collaboration with faculty at NPhD schools when there is an intellectual basis for it. Federal agencies can promote such collaboration in several ways, including encouraging and simplifying grant subcontracting. By exploiting the unique features of ECSE, greater research diversity and higher-quality education can be achieved.

## FACULTY EVALUATION

As noted above, research has only recently become a goal of NPhD schools, and the research tradition may not be strongly established. Thus, when evaluating a faculty member for promotion, senior faculty and administrators at NPhD schools, lacking decades of experience in assessing research and applying newly established policies, may be even more inclined to rely on raw "paper counts" than their peers at Ph.D.-granting institutions. This, of course, greatly jeopardizes ECSE faculty, who may have a modest publication list. Guidelines described elsewhere in this report should be applied when assessing ECSE faculty.

Realism must be applied in evaluating the accomplishments of junior ECSE faculty for tenure at NPhD schools: expectations must be in accord with circumstances. As already discussed, time is the most critical component of a junior faculty member's career. It must be possible to begin research quickly, there must be time to conduct the experimental work, and there will be a delay in the time between the artifact's or experiment's completion and the time the impact of the work is perceived. Resources—equipment, Internet connections, software, and so on—as well as students are critical to success. When assessing the faculty member's record and when requesting letters of evaluation, the constraints and circumstances that affected the faculty member's probationary period must be made explicit.

# 7

# Findings and Recommendations

The requirements for good research in experimental computer science and engineering (ECSE) are different from those of many other academic disciplines and require attention. Evaluation of such research likewise demands special attention because it differs from standard academic practice. Most significantly, the computational artifact is the medium of research in ECSE. The creation of an artifact often embodies a substantial portion of the intellectual contribution of experimental research and represents a significant intellectual effort. It is therefore important that the evaluation of ECSE research take proper account of the implications of the artifact as medium, as discussed in Chapters 1 and 2.

The importance of artifacts in demonstrating proofs of existence, concept, and performance in ECSE means that the development and implementation of computing artifacts with wide impact are comparable to the publication of papers with wide impact. In addition, the rapid pace of the ECSE field puts a high premium on timely communications. Because conferences are the vehicle of choice in ECSE for the dissemination of research, well-refereed conference proceedings (as well as work published in refereed private journals) should be given as much weight as archival journal articles in evaluating a candidate's research portfolio for promotion or tenure.

The infrastructure requirements of ECSE faculty are closer to those of the laboratory-based science and engineering disciplines than to those of the more theoretically oriented disciplines such as mathematics or statistics. Indeed, the committee believes that the lack of experimental infrastructure and/or a supportive research environment, including collaborators and mentors, may have greatly hampered or even prevented many talented experimentalists from producing significant research and thus led to their not receiving appropriate academic recognition. Reasonable expectations for research output should be scaled to match the resources available to an ECSE faculty member or team; this is especially important in light of the tighter funding picture for the foreseeable future.

The teaching dimension is problematic for many ECSE faculty, although differences among institutions of higher education obscure it to a certain degree. The very high student-faculty ratio in computer science and engineering (CS&E); the grading of complex student laboratory or project work in ECSE; the installation, maintenance, and upgrading of student ECSE laboratories; and keeping ECSE courses current in the face of rapidly changing technological underpinnings—all present extraordinarily time-intensive demands on ECSE faculty that should be recognized in making teaching assignments. The service dimension presents less of a problem, except for the rather frequent demand on ECSE faculty time to provide computer-related advice to the rest of the institution.

The focus on artifacts in ECSE, and other differences between the experimental and analytical methodologies, have led to tension between theoreticians and experimentalists. The manifestations of this tension vary from none at all in some departments to the perception, and perhaps the fact, in others that even very good junior experimental faculty members are being evaluated by criteria that are not appropriate for their research areas.

## RECOMMENDATIONS

The committee makes the following recommendations to improve the academic environment for ECSE.

### Recommendations for Departments

The importance of a supportive research environment for ECSE faculty cannot be overstated; indeed, it is so important that its absence may well defeat the most talented and gifted faculty member. Departments can help ECSE faculty, and especially new assistant professors, by

- Providing adequate "start-up" packages to ensure that resources are available to begin research immediately;
- Providing mentoring and advocacy, as described in Chapter 5;[1]
- Providing opportunities to teach advanced seminars in which graduate students can receive needed training in preparation for joining a research project;
- Considering mechanisms by which an assistant professor can move "off the tenure track" temporarily if research difficulties arise (while the tenure clock is ticking, assistant professors and their departments must be ever sensitive to the productive use of time);
- Explicitly encouraging collaborative work with like-minded colleagues wherever they may be found;
- Providing adequate teaching assistant support for time-intensive laboratory-based courses (teaching loads may also be adjusted when developing such courses); and
- Resolving matters related to potential intellectual property arrangements with industrially supported research or research undertaken jointly with industry.

In addition, departments must understand that high-quality ECSE research with great impact often demands a substantial commitment of resources. Departments that wish to maintain high-quality ECSE research programs must pay careful attention to the following:

- Equipment and equipment upgrades (which for state-of-the-art systems may be necessary as often as yearly);
- Equipment maintenance;
- Laboratory space;
- Technical staff, to keep the computing environment current;
- Software resources such as computer-aided design (CAD) tools; and
- Hardware resources such as networking and servers.

### Recommendations for University Evaluators

The six-year probationary period before most tenure decisions are made is short enough that even if a junior ECSE faculty member has structured his or her research so that significant intermediate results have been reported, the record is still likely to differ from

---

[1] Mentoring has received considerable attention in recent years as a vehicle for promoting greater diversity in CS&E departments. Mentoring and advocacy initiatives aimed at enhancing the careers of ECSE faculty should be harmonized with such efforts aimed at other important goals.

those of other academics, including theoretical computer scientists. This record may well contain fewer publications, fewer publications in archival journals, and more alternative forms of publication such as distributed software or other demonstrated artifacts.

The committee recognizes a wide range of approaches to evaluating candidates for tenure and promotion, and it does not wish to intrude on institutional prerogatives in determining how best to evaluate candidates. At the same time, the committee believes that evaluators should use standards and criteria that normally characterize productive work in the ECSE discipline, rather than standards that may be better aligned with more traditional academic disciplines, taking care not to exclude meaningful evidence of achievement simply because it is nonstandard (as discussed in Chapter 5.)

Evaluating artifacts is difficult, although certain data such as the number of users of a given artifact may provide some insight into the extent of its impact. Perhaps the best way to document impact, as well as other aspects of a person's research track record and potential, is to obtain informative letters of reference. Of course, the central question then becomes, Who should write letters for a candidate?

The committee believes that **the primary criteria in selecting a potential letter writer should be his or her stature in the field and familiarity with the candidate's work.** Other factors, such as the letter writer's institutional location or status as collaborator of the candidate, should not be cause for excluding letters from such individuals. In particular, because views from industry may be important for judging the impact of ECSE work, letters from individuals in industry or government should not be arbitrarily limited and should carry equal weight to those of similarly qualified and reputable individuals in academia.

## POLICY ISSUES

### Federal Government

Given the strong dependence of experimental computer scientists and engineers in academia on federal funding, it is obvious that federal funding policy can have a major impact on the field. Federal agencies that fund ECSE research may wish to take into account the following considerations:

• A variety of funding structures are needed to support ECSE research. These run the gamut from small, relatively short term grants or contracts that focus primarily on the elaboration of a concept, to large, relatively long term grants or contracts associated with deliverable computing artifacts. A good model of the latter is the National Science Foundation's Microelectronics Information Processing Systems (MIPS) program. Research initiation awards should continue. The committee recognizes the tightness of research budgets but points out that excessive trimming in the size or duration of individual research initiation awards will increase the risk that any given award will not lead to a significant ECSE research project.

• Computer science departments are major beneficiaries of tax policies that encourage computer manufacturers to donate computer equipment to universities. However, because the deductibility of such contributions is determined on the basis of the cost to manufacture the equipment, these same policies discourage the donation of software (because the "manufacturing" cost of software is not much more than the cost of copying a few tapes or disks). The committee does not have the expertise to comment fully on the ramifications of tax policy but points out that the manufacturing costs of software do not reflect R&D costs and understate the value of software from both technical and business perspectives.

• Given the long time scales necessary to establish reputations in ECSE, postdoctoral support for new Ph.D.s in ECSE would be especially beneficial. Two or three years of postdoctoral support in which new Ph.D.s could begin to develop a research program and style would enable them to "hit the ground running" upon taking an assistant professorship. More importantly, the artifacts on which their reputations are based would have additional time to propagate into the community.

### Industry

The computer and software industries in the United States have a direct and vested interest in the health of both the research and the educational dimensions of ECSE in academia. In addition, the spread of computer technology throughout business and industry, and the increasing sophistication of applications therein, suggest that firms in noncomputer industries—especially those that engage in significant applications development—also have a stake in ECSE. Thus, these industries may wish to take into account the following considerations:

• Academic ECSE research and education can be greatly enriched across the board by intellectual contact with industry. However, less well recognized schools find it especially difficult to establish collaborative work arrangements with industry. The committee points out that exposure of local computer science and engineering departments to the problems and needs of industry may result not only in meaningful collaborative work but also in students who are better informed about those problems. Such students graduating from less well recognized universities may be more likely to work for computer, software, or other computing-intensive companies near these universities.

• Academic ECSE research has benefited greatly from industrial donations of equipment. However, maintenance costs are often substantial, and university funds to cover such costs are in short supply. In some cases, donated technical support and maintenance may be worth as much to a university as a donated machine.

• The source code for a software system is essential for most meaningful experimental research on that system. An academic researcher's access to a needed source code will certainly reduce the time required for him or her to complete an experimental software system and may result in an improved system of direct interest to the owner of the source code. Of course, the researcher and the industrial provider of the source code will have to reach agreements that guard the interests of both (the researcher in being able to publish or present results of the research and the company in maintaining its competitive advantages from that software).

# Appendixes

# Appendix A
# Surveying the ECSE Community

In its deliberations, the Computer Science and Telecommunications Board (CSTB) Committee on Academic Careers for Experimental Computer Scientists made considerable use of several informal surveys of the experimental computer science and engineering (ECSE) community.

One survey was sent to the approximately 180 chairs of departments on the Forsythe list (i.e., all chairs of Ph.D.-granting departments in the United States and Canada in computer science and engineering (CS&E)); this questionnaire is presented as Exhibit A. Seventy department heads responded to this survey, of whom about 40 were themselves experimentalists. A second survey was sent to experimental computer scientists and engineers in academia identified through the procedure described in Box A.1; this questionnaire is presented as Exhibit B. A third survey was sent to graduate students in ECSE; this questionnaire is presented as Exhibit C. These students were identified by asking the ECSE faculty mentioned above to pass along the survey to their Ph.D. graduate students who had passed comprehensive exams. About 200 graduate students responded to the survey. (Because the committee had no way of knowing the number of Ph.D. graduate students working for the ECSE faculty members who received the questionnaire, the total number of graduate students who received the survey is not known.)

These surveys were developed and sent under the auspices of the

---

**BOX A.1 Identifying ECSE Faculty Members Through a "Friends-of-Friends" Procedure**

Approximately 900 individuals were identified by sending a short e-mail note to about a half-dozen individuals suggested by committee members, asking them to respond with the names and e-mail addresses of five other individuals in ECSE and employed in academic institutions. These names and addresses were recorded in a database, and the same note was sent to these individuals. The process was then iterated, with notes sent only to new individuals who were not already recorded in the database. By the time the process was terminated (on the basis of elapsed time—about 10 weeks), nearly 1,250 names had been generated. The figure of 900 given above is the number of individuals mentioned by two or more respondents. The electronic questionnaire was sent to the 900 individuals. Of these, about 220 responded, representing about 90 departments. The results of this procedure are presented more fully in Figure A.1.

This method for obtaining names was not comprehensive, in that a number of individuals personally known by the committee to fit the search criteria were not identified; these individuals were located at both less well known and better-known institutions. However, the committee believes that this method was able to generate coverage of a relatively large part of the ECSE community in a very short time and at negligible cost.

NOTE: Brian Reid, a member of the committee, brought this procedure to the committee's attention and was responsible for its implementation. In the time since this procedure was executed, the committee has learned that statisticians have known of this technique for a long time and refer to it as "snowball sampling."

---

Computing Research Association, a professional organization that represents the interests of the CS&E research community; however, answers were returned directly to committee staff. Of course, the analysis of data and the conclusions drawn from these surveys are entirely the responsibility of the committee.

Ideally, the committee would have conducted an ethnographic study of all institutions in which ECSE research is pursued and an analysis to distill common themes. Lacking the resources and the expertise to conduct a project of such dimensions, committee members decided on an approach that would yield as much information as possible. In particular, the information gathered by surveys was

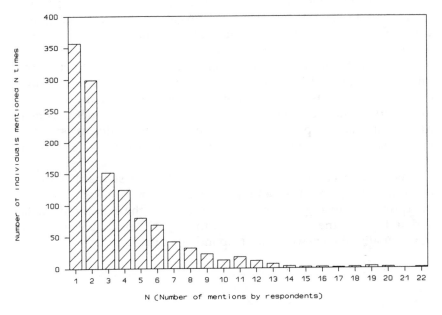

FIGURE A.1 Results of "friends-of-friends" polling for experimental computer scientists and engineers in academia.

used primarily as a reality check on the insights derived from the discussions of committee members with their colleagues.

Thus, although the committee believes that the surveys returned cover a considerable portion of the academic community of experimental computer scientists and engineers,[1] both tenure-track faculty and graduate students, it must point out that they do not constitute a complete or necessarily even a representative sample of the community, and biases are undoubtedly present in the responses. Perhaps the most serious bias is the fact that respondents may have been

---

[1] The total number of faculty in Ph.D.-granting computer science and engineering departments in 1989 was 2,660 (Computer Science and Telecommunications Board. 1992. *Computing the Future*, National Academy Press, Washington, D.C., p. 255), although the number of those conducting *experimental* computer science or engineering is unknown. It is the committee's qualitative impression that experimental computer scientists and engineers are, broadly speaking, in the minority across the nation. The total number of Ph.D. graduate students is also unknown, although it is known that some 800 graduate students receive Ph.D.s in computer science or engineering every year.

disproportionately more dissatisfied with their current status in academia than a true random sampling would reveal. At the same time, survey respondents included a number of the leading experimentalists in the field.

It would be misleading to present these survey results as being uniformly true for the entire ECSE community in academia. However, the comments of the respondents do represent the views of those individuals, and because the number of respondents constituted a substantial portion of the relevant community, it is fair to assert that their comments cannot be taken as isolated or aberrational.

As an inspection of the surveys indicates, questions that would result in both quantitative and qualitative data were asked. No clear interpretations emerged from a consideration of the quantitative data, and, in the end, the committee found that the richest data were found in the qualitative answers that respondents provided.

**Exhibit A: QUESTIONNAIRE SENT THROUGH U.S. MAIL TO DEPARTMENT HEADS**

## ABOUT YOURSELF AND YOUR DEPARTMENT

o    Your name _____

o    Your institution_____

o    Are you personally an experimental computer scientist or engineer? _____

o    How long have you been department head? _____

o    What is the total number of tenured and tenure-track faculty (i.e., funded by "hard money") in your department? _____

o    What is the total number of research-only faculty (i.e., funded by "soft money" but eligible for tenure) in your department? _____

o    Please indicate the extent to which it is an important departmental goal to maintain a presence in experimental computer science or engineering research. (1 = very important, 2 = somewhat important, 3 = not very important, 4 = not important at all)

      _____
       -

o    Please list the names and ranks of the faculty members in your department whom *you* consider to be experimental computer scientists or engineers. (An experimentalist in CS&E is one whose primary intellectual activities (outside of teaching) involve the actual construction of novel hardware or software systems, or the experimentation on or with such systems.) This information will be used simply to characterize the demographics of experimentalists, but will otherwise remain entirely private.

## FACULTY RECRUITMENT AND RETENTION

Please indicate the extent to which you believe there is a problem for your department in the areas listed below. Use the following scale in answering each question.

1 = an important problem that is generally very difficult to manage and handle

2 = an important problem, but one that can be managed or handled some but not all of the time

3 = a moderate problem, important only occasionally

4 = not much of a problem at all

**NOTE: ECSE refers to experimental computer science or engineering.**

A1- Attracting new PhDs in experimental CS&E . . . . . . . . . . . . . . . . . . . . . . 1 2 3 4

If you believe there is a problem in this area, please indicate the importance of the following possible reasons

    o competition from industry . . . . . . . . . . . . . . . . . . . . . . . . . . . . . . 1 2 3 4
    o competition from other universities  . . . . . . . . . . . . . . . . . . . . . . 1 2 3 4
    o availability of qualified applicants  . . . . . . . . . . . . . . . . . . . . . . 1 2 3 4
    o other (specify)_____  . . . . . . . . . . . . . . . 1 2 3 4

A2- Retaining faculty members in ECSE before the tenure decision is made  . . . 1 2 3 4

A3- Retaining faculty members in ECSE after the tenure decision is made  . . . . 1 2 3 4

A4- Promoting and/or reappointing faculty members in ECSE . . . . . . . . . . . . . . 1 2 3 4

If you believe there is a problem in this area, please indicate the importance of the following possible reasons:

    o   difficulties in evaluating the fundamental contributions
        made by experimental work . . . . . . . . . . . . . . . . . . . . . . . . . . . 1 2 3 4
    o   tensions between experimentalists and theorists  . . . . . . . . . . . . 1 2 3 4
    o   difficulties in evaluating collaborative work  . . . . . . . . . . . . . . . 1 2 3 4
    o   excessive time needed for setting up
        teaching or research laboratories in ECSE . . . . . . . . . . . . . . . . 1 2 3 4
    o   excessive time needed to perform research in ECSE  . . . . . . . . . 1 2 3 4
    o   other (specify)_____  . . . . . . . . . . . . . . . . . . . . . . . . . 1 2 3 4


A5- Obtaining university sanction for making research contacts with industry  . . 1 2 3 4

A6- Obtaining university sanction for projects in ECSE  . . . . . . . . . . . . . . . . . 1 2 3 4

A7- Providing a good research environment for faculty members in ECSE . . . . . 1 2 3 4

If you believe there is a problem in this area, please indicate the importance of the following possible reasons:

    o obtaining funding for research in ECSE  . . . . . . . . . . . . . . . . . . . . 1 2 3 4
    o obtaining staff support for ECSE
        (e.g., programmers, technicians) . . . . . . . . . . . . . . . . . . . . . . . . 1 2 3 4
    o obtaining graduate students interested
        in ECSE  . . . . . . . . . . . . . . . . . . . . . . . . . . . . . . . . . . . . . . . . 1 2 3 4
    o other (specify)
        _____  . . . . . . . . . . . . 1 2 3 4

A8- Faculty attrition. Please fill in the table below, counting as a departure an individual in a tenured or tenure-track position in experimental computer science or engineering (ECSE) that left your department in the last ten years. Include both regular faculty and research-only faculty.

| TOTAL NUMBER OF ECSE DEPARTURES IN LAST 10 YEARS | After being denied tenure | After receiving tenure (COLUMN A) | Before receiving tenure, but unlikely to have received tenure (COLUMN B) | Before receiving tenure, but likely to have received tenure (COLUMN C) |
|---|---|---|---|---|
| | | | | |

Generalizing to the extent possible from the cases in the last three columns (Columns A, B, and C), what do you believe have been their reasons for leaving academia? Please use the following scale to indicate the relative importance of the factors below.

1 = important to most or all of the cases in question

2 = important to some of the cases in question

3 = important only to a few or none of the cases in question

If you feel it is necessary, please include a note about the degree of impact of these factors on the decisions in question.

| | Column ==>> | A | B | C |
|---|---|---|---|---|
| better pay in industry | | | | |
| better access to resources in industry | | | | |
| better opportunity for impact in industry | | | | |
| more professional recognition in industry | | | | |
| better intellectual environment in industry | | | | |
| better opportunities at another university | | | | |
| academic career not going well | | | | |
| deciding that academic career was not right for them | | | | |

## EXPERIMENTAL COMPUTER SCIENCE AND ENGINEERING IN YOUR DEPARTMENT

B1- Please rank the adequacy of various components of your institution's infrastructure for the teaching and training of graduate students in ECSE and for your faculty's research.

| 1 = superb | 3 = adequate |
| 2 = very good | 4 = inadequate |

| Adequacy of infrastructure component listed below for: | teaching and training of graduate students in ECSE | research by ECSE faculty |
|---|---|---|
| hardware | | |
| software | | |
| technical non-student support (e.g., programmers) | | |
| space | | |
| time (before tenure decision is made or before student is "taking too long") | | |
| supply of qualified graduate students (only for faculty) | | |
| administrative support (only for faculty) | | |

B2- What is the largest experimental project your department has undertaken in the last 10 years? (Please use your best estimate if it is inconvenient to gather data.)

| Total Person-years (FTE) expended | Total funding expended | Brief Description |
|---|---|---|
| | | |

B3- Using your best estimate, please fill in the following table on your department's ECSE research projects in the last 10 years.

| Category of ECSE Project | Number in Last 10 Years |
|---|---|
| Total Number of ECSE Projects | |
| Project depended on industrially donated or industrially subsidized equipment. | |
| Project received a substantial degree of industry funding (i.e., over 30% of total project funding from industry, but not including donated or subsidized equipment). | |
| Project was/is "large" (i.e., over $1.5 M in total budget, over 12 person years in total effort). | |
| Project was/is "medium" (i.e., between $500 K and $1.5 M in total budget, between 6 and 12 person years in total effort). | |
| Project was/is "small" (i.e., under $500 K in total budget, less than 6 person years in total effort, but still involving the construction of or experimentation with a hardware or software system). | |

B4- Peers/Mentors and Collaboration among Experimental Computer Scientists and Engineers

Using this scale,

1 = adequate or better for most ECSE faculty
2 = adequate or better for some ECSE faculty

3 = adequate or better for only a few or no ECSE faculty

please give us your assessment of:

-- the mentoring support provided by your department for
its junior experimental computer scientists and engineers ................... 1  2  3

-- the opportunities provided by your department for collaboration
among your experimental computer scientists and engineers (both junior
and senior faculty) ............................................... 1  2  3

B5- Evaluation Procedures

For each of the following items in a faculty member's evaluation portfolio, give its approximate percentage weight of importance in your institution's evaluation of his or her research. Please ensure that your weights total to 100%.

___ a. letters
     ___ a.1 - from industry
     ___ a.2 - from universities
        (Entries for a.1 and a.2 should sum to the entry for a.)
___ b. published contributions
     ___ b.1 - in refereed conference proceedings
     ___ b.2 - in archival journals
        (Entries for b.1 and b.2 should sum to the entry for b.)
___ c. implementation of hardware/software artifacts (not described in published contributions)

___ d. patents or copyrights

B6- How difficult does your department find it to evaluate collaborative work in tenure and promotion cases? (check one)

___ difficult in most or all cases                ___ never difficult or difficult in only a few cases
___ difficult in some cases

## YOUR GRADUATE PROGRAM

C1- Please fill in the following table about the graduate students in your department.

| Total number of Ph.D. students in your department | Number of Ph.D. students in ECSE | Number of ECSE Ph.D. students supported by teaching assistantship | Number of ECSE Ph.D. students supported by research assistantship | Number of ECSE Ph.D. students supported by fellowship |
|---|---|---|---|---|
| | | | | |

C2- Describe in a sentence or two any general requirement for all Ph.D. students to fulfill some type of experimental computer science or engineering (e.g., work on a system, build a piece of hardware, take a course in experimental methods in ECSE).

**Please make any additional comments you wish on an additional sheet of paper.** Otherwise, thanks for your help.

**Exhibit B**: QUESTIONNAIRE SENT ELECTRONICALLY TO SYSTEMS FACULTY MEMBERS ON JULY 9, 1992

Dear systems faculty member:

The Computer Science and Telecommunications Board (CSTB) of the National Research Council (NRC) is conducting a study on the difficulties encountered by experimental computer scientists and engineers in pursuing academic careers. The Computing Research Association is assisting with this study.

Some people believe that experimental computer scientists are handicapped in academia because the nature of their work (for example, the construction of large computer hardware or software systems, or experimentation with or on such systems) is fundamentally different from the work pursued in more traditional disciplines. Such differences might lead to difficulties in promotion and tenure or influence choices regarding research problems. Others believe that there is no problem unique to experimental computer science and engineering.

Your name was selected in a sampling of university faculty members in experimental computer science or engineering, and we'd like to ask you some questions that would help to shed light on this subject. Also, we've included a questionnaire for you to pass on to your Ph.D. graduate students who have passed their qualifying exams. Your answers and those of your students will help to guide the deliberations of the study committee, which will produce its report by the Spring of 1993; you will of course receive a free copy of the report at that time.

This questionnaire should take no more than a half hour or so of your time. We ask you some questions about events since you joined your department; your general recollections should be sufficient, and will enable a more prompt response.

NRC reports are often highly influential in the Washington policy community, and the findings and recommendations of this report may well have impact on our field as a whole. I urge you to respond to this inquiry by August 10, 1992. If you have any questions about the questionnaire, please contact the Computer Science and Telecommunications Board at the telephone number or net address below.

We recognize that some of the information you are asked to provide may be sensitive, and we wish to assure you that all responses will be used for the purposes of this study only, and no information will be used in a way that allows your personal or institutional identification without your explicit permission. If you have any questions, please contact the CSTB. You may send your response directly to HLIN@NAS.EDU.

Thanks in advance for any help you can offer. Your cooperation is very much appreciated.

Sincerely,

John Rice
Professor of Computer Science, Purdue University
Board Chair, Computing Research Association

Larry Snyder
Professor of Computer Science, University of Washington
Chairman, NRC Committee on Academic Careers for Experimental Computer
Scientists

================= QUESTIONNAIRE ======================
THIS QUESTIONNAIRE IS DESIGNED TO BE ANSWERED USING AN ON-LINE
TEXT EDITOR. IF YOU CHOOSE TO ANSWER IT OFFLINE IN HARDCOPY,
YOU MAY WISH TO INCREASE THE NUMBER OF BLANK LINES FOLLOWING
CERTAIN QUESTIONS TO HAVE ADEQUATE SPACE FOR A RESPONSE.
=============================================================

1 -- ABOUT YOURSELF

1.a- Your name_____

1.b- Your Department/Institution_____

1.c- Your Rank and Title_____

1.d- How many years have you been in your department?_____

1.e- What fraction of your professional career in the last 10 years has
been spent in research?_____

1.f- What fraction of your research effort in the past 10 years has been
devoted to the actual construction of hardware or software systems,
the experimentation on or with such systems, or the supervision of
students engaged in these activities?_____

1.g- If a tenure decision has been made for you, how has that decision
changed the character of your research? If one has not been made yet
for you, how do you expect it to do so? Please explain why in either
case.

2 -- YOUR PH.D. STUDENTS

Please give us some information about the Ph.D. graduate students for whom
you have been the advisor of record and who have received their doctorates
in the last 10 years. (Using your best memory on the subject will be
adequate, though if you can check records without too much trouble, we
encourage you to do so.)

2.1. For the student you rank 1 (your best) among all your graduates,
indicate:

Year Ph.D. awarded:

Thesis area:

Name of student's first employer after Ph.D.:

If this student is presently working in industry, what factors influenced his/her decision?  (check)

___ better environment in industry (specify how, e.g., research  money,
equipment, colleagues)
___ couldn't get or unlikely to get tenure
___ unable to find suitable academic job
___ unable to find any academic job
___ other (specify)

2.2.  For the student you rank 2 (your second best) among all your
graduates, indicate:

Year Ph.D. awarded:

Thesis area:

Name of student's first employer after Ph.D.:

If this student is presently working in industry, what factors
influenced his/her decision?  (check)

___ better environment in industry (specify how, e.g., research  money,
equipment, colleagues)
___ couldn't get or unlikely to get tenure
___ unable to find suitable academic job
___ unable to find any academic job
___ other (specify)


2.3.  For the student you rank 3 (your third best) among all your
graduates, indicate:

Year Ph.D. awarded:

Thesis area:

Name of student's first employer after Ph.D.:

If this student is presently working in industry, what factors
influenced his/her decision?  (check)

___ better environment in industry (specify how, e.g., research  money,
equipment, colleagues)
___ couldn't get or unlikely to get tenure
___ unable to find suitable academic job
___ unable to find any academic job
___ other (specify)

2.4 through 2.n [Please replicate above text for the remainder of your
Ph.D. students.]

3 -- YOUR FACULTY COLLEAGUES

3.a- Success Factors in Experimental Computer Science and Engineering

In successful tenure or promotion cases for experimental computer scientists and engineers, what factors were most important? Evaluate according to the following scale:

1 = important to most or all of the cases in question
2 = important to some of the cases in question
3 = important to only a few or none of the cases in question

____ letters from industry
____ letters from senior experimental researchers in academia
____ letters from senior non-experimental researchers in academia
____ publications record
____ evidence of contributions other than publications (specify)
____ impact on industry
____ other (specify) _____

3.b- Faculty Arrivals: please consider as an "arrival" a person hired into a tenured or tenure-track in experimental computer science or engineering (ECSE). Include regular faculty (those with research and teaching responsibilities) and tenure-eligible research-only faculty without regular teaching responsibilities. If you have been in your department for less than 10 years, please answer for the number of years you have been in your department. (Your best recollection will be adequate, though if you can check records without too much trouble, we encourage you to do so.)


ECSE ARRIVALS IN LAST 10 YEARS: Arriving fresh out of graduate school or from post-doc:

____ Number of new regular faculty hired with tenure
____ Number of new regular faculty hired without tenure
____ Number of new research-only faculty hired without tenure
____ Number of new research-only faculty hired without tenure


ECSE ARRIVALS IN LAST 10 YEARS: Arriving from faculty position in another university:

____ Number of new regular faculty hired with tenure
____ Number of new regular faculty hired without tenure
____ Number of new research-only faculty hired without tenure
____ Number of new research-only faculty hired without tenure

ECSE ARRIVALS IN LAST 10 YEARS: Arriving from industry:

____ Number of new regular faculty hired with tenure
____ Number of new regular faculty hired without tenure
____ Number of new research-only faculty hired without tenure
____ Number of new research-only faculty hired without tenure


3.c- Faculty Departures: please consider a departure an individual who left a tenured or tenure-track position in experimental computer science or engineering (ECSE). Include both regular faculty and research-only faculty. If you have been in your department for less than 10 years, please answer for the number of years you have been in your department.

___ TOTAL NUMBER OF ECSE DEPARTURES IN LAST 10 YEARS
___ After being denied tenure
___ After receiving tenure (CATEGORY A)
___ Before receiving tenure, but unlikely to have received tenure (CATEGORY B)
___ Before receiving tenure, but likely to have received tenure (CATEGORY C)

Generalizing to the extent possible from the cases in the last three categories (A, B, and C), what do you believe have been their reasons for leaving academia? Please use the following scale to indicate the relative importance of the factors below.

1 = important to most or all of the cases in question
2 = important to some of the cases in question
3 = important only to a few or none of the cases in question

If you feel it is necessary, please include a note about the DEGREE of impact of these factors on the decisions in question.

| | | | |
|---|---|---|---|
| better pay in industry | A.____ | B.____ | C.____ |
| better access to resources in industry | A.____ | B.____ | C.____ |
| better opportunity for impact in industry | A.____ | B.____ | C.____ |
| more professional recognition in industry | A.____ | B.____ | C.____ |
| better intellectual environment in industry | A.____ | B.____ | C.____ |
| better opportunities at another university | A.____ | B.____ | C.____ |
| academic career not going well | A.____ | B.____ | C.____ |
| deciding that academic career was not right for them | A.____ | B.____ | C.____ |

3.d- Tenure and Promotion (T/P) Cases for Experimental Computer Scientists and Engineers

Please include both regular faculty and research-only faculty eligible for tenure.

NOTE: If you have been in your department for less than 10 years, please answer for the number of years you have been in your department.

_____ total number of T/P cases in last 10 years (all parts of computer
      science and engineering)
_____ total number of T/P cases in ECSE
_____ total number of T/P cases in ECSE that were denied tenure
_____ number of denials in ECSE that you think were inappropriate

Generalizing from the cases in the last row (i.e., those unsuccessful cases that should, in your judgment, have been successful), what were the factors contributing to the cases' lack of success? Indicate their relative importance according to the following scale:

1 = important to most or all of the cases in question
2 = important to some of the cases in question
3 = important to only a few or none of the cases in question

____ lack of publications
____ lack of research funding
____ lack of Ph.D. students
____ classroom teaching problems
____ problems with advising students
____ difficulty in evaluating "artifacts" or contributions other than
     publications
____ personal relationships between candidate and department
____ lack of appropriate mentoring from senior faculty
____ lack of students to perform research
____ difficulty of evaluating interdisciplinary or cross-departmental
     research
____ lack of knowledge to pursue some research opportunity
____ poor handling of tenure case by department
____ mismatch between faculty members' goals and metrics commonly used for
     evaluation
____ lack of a relationship with industry
____ too much industrial interaction
____ inadequate equipment infrastructure
____ lack of staff support (e.g., programmers, technicians)
____ other (specify) _____

4 -- OTHER QUESTIONS

4.a- What is the dissemination channel you prefer for your work from the
     standpoint of MAXIMUM INTELLECTUAL IMPACT? Please rank order the
     following channels, where 1 is your most preferred channel.

     _____ conference proceedings    _____ archival journals
     _____ technical reports         _____ other (specify)

4.b- For your #1 choice above, why is that your most preferred dissemination channel?

4.c- What is the dissemination channel you prefer for your work from the standpoint of UNIVERSITY RECOGNITION? Please rank order the following channels, where 1 is your most preferred channel.

____ conference proceedings  ____ archival journals
____ technical reports  ____ other (specify)

4.d- For your #1 choice above, why is that your most preferred dissemination channel?

4.e- What advice would you give an incoming assistant professor who expresses an interest in doing experimental computer science?

4.f- Would you recommend an academic career in experimental computer science or engineering for a new graduate student today? Why or why not?

4.g- If any experimentalists stayed after being denied tenure, to what career track did they move?

4.h- Please add anything else you wish below. Otherwise, thanks for your help.

**Exhibit C: QUESTIONNAIRE FOR GRADUATE STUDENTS**

Dear doctoral student:

The Computer Science and Telecommunications Board (CSTB) of the National Research Council (NRC) is conducting a study on the difficulties encountered by experimental computer scientists and engineers in pursuing academic careers. The Computing Research Association is assisting with this study.

Some people believe that experimental computer scientists are handicapped in academia because the nature of their work (for example, the construction of large computer hardware or software systems, or experimentation with or on such systems) is fundamentally different from the work pursued in more traditional disciplines. Such differences might lead to difficulties in promotion and tenure or influence choices regarding research problems. Others believe that there is no problem unique to experimental computer science and engineering.

Your advisor was selected in a sampling of university faculty members to answer a few questions about academic careers in computer science and engineering. We are interested in your perceptions of academic careers in experimental computer science. Please answer the following questions and return your responses directly to: HLIN@NAS.EDU   If you have any questions, please contact the CSTB at the address given below.

Thanks in advance for any help you can offer. Your cooperation is very much appreciated.

Sincerely,

John Rice
Professor of Computer Science, Purdue University
Board Chair, Computing Research Association

Larry Snyder
Professor of Computer Science, University of Washington
Chair, NRC Committee on Academic Careers for Experimental Computer Scientists

1.  Do you consider yourself an experimental computer scientist? What do you think differentiates experimental from non-experimental work in computer science or engineering?

2.  What type of position do you plan to seek after graduation? Rank by order of preference (1 = most preferable)

    ____ academia (research-oriented university)

    \_\_\_ academia (teaching-oriented university)
    \_\_\_ industrial research laboratory\_\_\_ other industry
    \_\_\_ self-employed\_\_\_ government
    \_\_\_ other (specify)_____

3.   After you graduate, in what activities do you expect that you will spend your professional time? Please provide approximate percentages below:

\_\_\_\_ teaching
\_\_\_\_ doing experimental research that involves constructing hardware or software systems
\_\_\_\_ doing non-experimental research
\_\_\_\_ doing product development
\_\_\_\_ other (specify)

4.   What do you see as the primary minuses FOR YOU of seeking or taking academic positions in experimental computer science or engineering? (Please use the following scale in answering.)

   1 = very much a minus
   2 = something of a minus
   3 = not much of a minus
   4 = not at all a minus

\_\_ a. difficulty of getting tenure in university
\_\_ b. lack of adequate infrastructure for experimental work
\_\_ c. too much teaching
\_\_ d. too much emphasis on need to publish
\_\_ e. too much emphasis on need to raise funds for research
\_\_ f. salaries too low
\_\_ g. too hard to find university position in good location
\_\_ h. too hard to generate an academic job offer
\_\_ i. academic work has too little practical result or influence
\_\_ j. too difficult to do collaborative work at university
\_\_ k. inadequate intellectual community for my interests
\_\_ l. inadequate professional respect at university
\_\_ m. other (specify)_____

5.   What do you see as the primary pluses FOR YOU of seeking or taking academic positions in experimental computer science or engineering? (Please use the following scale in answering.)

   1 = very much a plus
   2 = something of a plus
   3 = not much of a plus
   4 = not at all a plus

\_\_ a. possibility of getting lifetime tenure
\_\_ b. oppportunity to teach

__ c. freedom to choose own topics of professional interest
__ d. opportunity to ignore commercial influences on research
__ e. opportunity to do cutting-edge state-of-the-art work
__ f. opportunities for intellectual collaboration
__ g. opportunity to work in an intellectually diverse environment
__ h. opportunity to supervise graduate student research
__ i. greater professional stature at university
__ j. other (specify)_____

6.    Please tell us anything else you wish below.

# Appendix B
# Comparing Journal and
# Conference Publication

This appendix compares several different quantitative measures of the acceptance and refereeing process (i.e., timeliness and selectivity) to determine how well the different publication media achieve the goals that experimental computer science and engineers desire, how these publication media might be improved, and what these publications tell us about the success of various academic researchers.

## TIME TO PUBLICATION

As mentioned earlier, long delays to publication are a major hindrance to progress in experimental computer science and engineering (ECSE).[1] Long publication delays also affect recognition and can be a problem in considering tenure and promotion cases. Journal editors try their best to minimize delay but are often stymied in their efforts by referees who do not return reviews in a timely fashion. The committee examined the time from submission to acceptance and publication for a variety of leading conferences and journals.

Table B.1 presents the times from submission to acceptance to publication for some major conferences; by comparison, the times for

---

[1] The circulation of preprints in ECSE is extensive (assisted in rapid distribution by connections to the Internet) and testifies to a problem with timeliness.

TABLE B.1   Time from Submission to Acceptance and
Publication of Papers for Selected Conferences and Journals

|  | Time to Acceptance (months) | Time to Publication (months) |
|---|---|---|
| Conference[a] | | |
| PLDI | 2.3 | 7.3 |
| ISCA | 2.6 | 6.2 |
| ASPLOS | 2.5 | 7.0 |
| SOSP | 3.0 | 7.8 |
| OOPSLA | 2.6 | 7.2 |
| SIGGRAPH | 2.3 | 6.8 |
| Average | 2.5 | 7.0 |
| Journal[b] | | |
| TOPLAS | 24.0 | 32.4 |
| TOCS | 17.0 | 21.3 |
| IEEE TOC | N/A | 32.2 |
| IEEE TSE | N/A | 29.2 |

[a]PLDI, conference on Programming Language Design and Implementation; ISCA, International Symposium on Computer Architecture; ASPLOS, conference on Architectural Support for Programming Languages and Operating Systems; SOSP, Symposium on Operating System Principles; OOPSLA, conference on Object-Oriented Programming Systems, Languages, and Applications; SIGGRAPH, conference of the ACM Special Interest Group on Graphics.

[b]TOPLAS, *Transactions on Programming Languages and Systems* (published by ACM); TOCS, *Transactions on Computer Systems* (published by ACM); TOC, *Transactions on Computers* (published by IEEE; data for 1988 to 1992, special issues omitted); and TSE, *Transactions on Software Engineering* (published by IEEE; data for 1988 to 1992, special issues omitted).

journal submission and publication are much longer. Table B.1 also indicates the comparable times for two of the primary Association of Computing Machinery (ACM) journals that publish ECSE research. Notice that the conferences listed, except for ASPLOS, are annual and the journals quarterly.

For *Transactions on Programming Languages and Systems* (TOPLAS), it takes approximately 10 times longer to acceptance and 5 times longer to publication than conferences require, whereas *Transactions on Computer Systems* (TOCS) requires about 6 times longer for acceptance and 2.7 times longer for publication than conferences. (For TOCS the average was significantly reduced by the use of special issues that offered fast-track publication to selected, top-rated conference papers.)

Multiple sequences of refereeing and revision account for a large

## TABLE B.2  Publication Time and Manuscript Revision History for TOPLAS

| Revisions Required | Fraction of Submissions (%) | Time to Acceptance (months) | Time to Publication (months) |
|---|---|---|---|
| 1 | 50 | 18.0 | 26.4 |
| 2 | 45 | 30.0 | 37.2 |
| 3 | 5 | 37.2 | 46.8 |

## TABLE B.3  Age of References in Journal and Conference Publications

| Publication[a] | Fraction of References to Papers Less Than Two Years Old (%) | Median Age of Reference (years) |
|---|---|---|
| ASPLOS (Conference) | 32 | 3 |
| ISCA (Conference) | 35 | 3 |
| PLDI (Conference) | 26 | 4 |
| TOCS (Journal) | 20 | 4.5 |
| TOPLAS (Journal) | 12 | 5 |

[a]ASPLOS, conference on Architectural Support for Programming Languages and Operating Systems; ISCA, International Symposium on Computer Architecture; PLDI, conference on Programming Language Design and Implementation; TOCS, *Transactions on Computer Systems* (published by ACM); TOPLAS, *Transactions on Programming Languages and Systems* (published by ACM).

part of the delay in journal publication. For example, Table B.2 presents data from three years of TOPLAS. Even if only the 50 percent of submissions that require merely one revision are considered, journal acceptance requires about 6 times longer, and publication 3.7 times longer, than the average conference, which confirms that conferences offer a substantial advantage in timeliness.

With the rapid advances in experimental computer science, timeliness is critical. One way of seeing how important timeliness is and how it is affected by publication time is to look at the citations in published papers.

Table B.3 contains data computed from looking at all the references in an entire year for TOCS and TOPLAS plus all the references in one year's ASPLOS, ISCA, and PLDI conferences. From these data, it is clear that the longer selection and publication process of journals means that they cannot be as current as conference publications.   Rather than having about 30 percent of their references to recent papers (last two years), journals have on average only about 16 percent of their references to papers this recent.   The average age of a reference is also older.

One of the reasons often given (by researchers as well as university administrators) for preferring journal over conference publication is the more critical reviewing and more permanent record offered by the former. If the journal papers were more critically reviewed and therefore of higher quality, it might be expected that they would be cited significantly more frequently than conference papers.

However, this is not borne out by the data. For example, among conferences the citations to other conference papers outnumber the citations to journals by 1.6 to 1 (45 percent versus 28 percent). Although the citations among journal papers are evenly divided, this appears to reflect the much older median age of a citation. For example, among the conference papers with citations older than four years, the citations to journal and conference papers are also evenly balanced. Thus, it appears that many researchers do not perceive a significant difference in quality or importance between conference and journal publication.

It is worth noting that a positive feedback loop may have occurred in ECSE.  In particular, the need for rapid publication has driven many academic experimentalists away from journal publication, perhaps resulting in a reduction of the pressure on journals to publish.[2]  By contrast, other fast-moving disciplines make use of journals with rapid publication times; an informal survey of materials science and biotechnology journals indicates mean publication times on the order of several months, rather than the years that characterize CS&E journals.

## SELECTIVITY

Among the smaller fraction of experimental computer science researchers who favored journal publication over conference publication (approximately one-quarter of the respondents to the survey in Appendix A), nearly half listed the more critical reviewing of journals as their motivation.

Although the journal reviewing process may be more thorough,

---

[2] This is not to say that journal editors are satisfied with the speed with which journal articles can be refereed, revised, and ultimately published—quite the contrary is true.

TABLE B.4  Acceptance Rates for Selected Conferences (%)

| Conference[a] | Year 1 | Year 2 | Year 3 | Average |
|---|---|---|---|---|
| SIGGRAPH | 21 | 19 | 20 | 20 |
| ASPLOS | 24 | 30 | 16 | 23 |
| ISCA | 14 | 19 | 23 | 19 |
| PLDI | 17 | 17 | 17 | 18 |

[a]SIGGRAPH, conference of the ACM Special Interest Group on Graphics; ASPLOS, conference on Architectural Support for Programming Languages and Operating Systems; ISCA, International Symposium on Computer Architecture; PLDI, conference on Programming Language Design and Implementation.

the prestigious conferences are highly selective. Table B.4 shows the acceptance rates for the last three occurrences of several top experimental conferences (ASPLOS is biennial, whereas the others are annual).

It is much harder to determine the acceptance rates for journals, because comparable statistics are not kept and the long reviewing process makes it difficult to determine the final outcome of a paper. The committee did examine the submission and publication rates for TOPLAS and found that the average acceptance rate over a five-year period was 27 percent of the papers submitted (this includes revised papers). An informal survey of editors of other major ACM and Institute of Electrical and Electronics Engineers (IEEE) journals found acceptance rates that vary from about 25 to 35 percent. The private journals tend to be in the same range, although at the higher end.